Touching the Core

My quest to become a leader

Dr. Subhashis Chakraborty

INDIA · SINGAPORE · MALAYSIA

ISBN

Hardcase 979-8-89961-525-2
Paperback 979-8-89961-524-5

Dedication

This book is first and foremost dedicated to the guiding lights of my life, my parents.

To my father, Mr. Debashis Chakraborty, now residing in the heavenly abode, whose silent presence continues to inspire me every day. His unwavering commitment, sacrifices, and remarkable resilience shaped the person I am today. He was not just a father, but a mentor who walked the talk and taught me the value of patience and persistence. It was he who gave me the freedom to make my own choices and follow my own path, empowering me to shape my own destiny. But above all, it was the unmistakable pride in his eyes that lit the fire in me—the drive to become someone you'd always be proud of. Even now, that image of him, smiling with quiet joy at my smallest wins, continues to fuel my passion to strive higher, do better, and never stop growing.

To my mother, Mrs. Tripti Chakraborty, whose love is boundless and whose wisdom is immeasurable. She is the very soul within me, the foundation of my strength and courage. It's her love and her teachings that have nourished me throughout my life, helping me face the world with pride, purpose, and a heart full of hope. I feel truly blessed to have her as my greatest coach and guiding star.

But no story of mine would be whole without the one who makes me whole—my soulmate, Dr. Dali. She is not just my partner, but my mirror, my anchor, and the quiet strength behind my boldest strides. With her, I've discovered the courage to grow, the grace to endure, and the joy of shared victories. She doesn't just walk beside me—she is the path beneath my feet. Life, in its fullest meaning, begins and blossoms with her.

It was only when I became a parent that I truly understood the depth, the joy, and the quiet strength it takes to raise a child. To my amazing, sweet daughters, Shreshtha and Pratishtha—my radiant, innocent angels—thank you for filling my world with curiosity, laughter, and boundless love. Shreshtha, your fierce determination, and drive to succeed makes me pause and reflect; Pratishtha, your unwavering kindness and bright smile lifts me even on the hardest days. You inspire me every single day to become a better version of myself. Your love, your little victories, and the sparkle you bring to life breathe meaning into every word of this book.

To my wonderful brother, Tony, and lovely sister-in-law, Debkanya—thank you for being the steady pillars in my life. Your unwavering belief in me has been a quiet force of strength, lifting me through challenges and cheering me on in moments of triumph. I am deeply grateful for the unconditional love, respect, and warmth you bring into my world—it means more than words can express.

I also owe a tremendous debt of gratitude to my incredible team— Ganesh, Shincy, Uma, Priyanka, and Sahil. Your unconditional commitment, relentless dedication and trust in me have been the backbone of this journey. From steering complex product launches to championing innovation in projects, you've exemplified the true meaning of collaboration and the power of purpose-driven teamwork. I am because of you—and this book is as much yours as it is mine.

To all my managers, mentors, and colleagues, both past and present—whether you directly or indirectly contributed to my leadership journey—thank you. Your wisdom, guidance, and at times, the tough lessons, have all played a part in shaping me into the leader I am today. I am deeply grateful for the impact you've had on my personal and professional growth.

And lastly, to my readers—you have entrusted me with your hearts, your time, and your thoughts. Your belief in me, your silent companionship through these pages, and your willingness to reflect, feel, and grow alongside my words—have made this journey meaningful. Your love and curiosity have fuelled my desire to share not just a story, but a part of my soul. Thank you for walking this path with me.

*I dedicate this book, **Touching the Core - My Quest to Become a Leader**, to each of you. May you all find inspiration in these pages, as you have inspired me throughout my life.*

Contents

Preface

Over the years, I've found myself returning to one simple truth: happiness is not an outcome—it's a way of being. In my earlier books - **Happiness D'Coded** and **Womb to Grave**, I tried to unravel that truth—not from a scholar's podium, but from the messy yet simple and ordinary yet beautiful spaces of everyday life.

I've never claimed to be an expert. My writing has always come from lived experiences—watching people, making mistakes, listening quietly, sometimes failing, sometimes healing, and learning constantly. Whether it was choosing peace over ego in a petty argument or reminding myself to let go of frustration when a small error didn't go my way—every moment taught me a little more about what truly matters.

In this book, the conversation shifts. Not away from happiness— but toward a place where happiness and responsibility meet: **LEADERSHIP.**

Leadership, like happiness, isn't about perfection. It's not reserved for those with titles or corner offices. It's about how we show up—for ourselves and for others. It's about owning our energy, our influence, and our impact. Just as personal joy is built on simple, conscious choices, great leadership is forged in everyday decisions—how we treat people, how we respond to pressure, how we grow, how we forgive, and how we inspire.

Too often, leaders are burdened by metrics, expectations, and the illusion of control. But the most admired leaders—the ones who shape lives, not just balance sheets—are those who lead with authenticity, humility, and heart. They understand that people don't follow titles; they follow values. They see the bigger picture and the smallest gesture. They recognize that leadership is not about power, but purpose.

This book is not a rulebook. It's a reflection. A collection of thoughts, insights, and reminders to bring leadership back to where it belongs: in our humanity. It's about knowing when to take charge and when to step back, when to speak and when to listen, when to push and when to pause.

I hope that as you turn these pages, you'll find ideas that resonate—not because they're revolutionary, but because they're real. My goal isn't to impress you with jargon or frameworks. It's to remind you of what you already know deep down—that the best leaders are, first and foremost, good humans.

Leadership doesn't begin at the top. It begins within. Let's begin....

Introduction

In my earlier works—**Happiness D'Coded** and **Womb to Grave**—I explored the intricate dance between personal fulfillment and the pursuit of happiness amid life's complexities. Both books revealed a fundamental truth: happiness and success are not opposing forces but rather deeply interconnected paths to a meaningful life.

Happiness D'Coded shed light on the everyday struggle of individuals trying to reconcile personal dreams with societal and familial responsibilities. While we often look to spiritual gurus or iconic entrepreneurs for inspiration, the reality is that most people grapple with achieving contentment and success simultaneously. Through personal anecdotes and practical insights, the book offered strategies to strike this balance—without compromising ambition or well-being.

In **Womb to Grave**, I delved deeper into the timeless quest for happiness in a world increasingly driven by speed and noise. Drawing from the wisdom of thinkers like Rabindranath Tagore, the book reminded readers that while happiness is inherently simple, our pursuit of it is often complicated by societal expectations, external validation, and a growing disconnection from our inner selves. It encouraged introspection, simplicity, and a return to what truly matters.

I've been writing about happiness for quite some time—not based on any formal training, but drawn from life's lessons, gathered through experiences, keen observation, and common sense. My reflections have been shaped by the wisdom I've gained from insightful people I've met across my career, from real-life situations, from thought-provoking books, and from personal incidents in my own professional journey. I've intentionally kept the narrative simple—so that it's not just easy to read, but also easy to implement in everyday life.

Sometimes, the biggest truth comes from the smallest moments:

If my spouse forgets to pick up something important from the store, should I sulk in silence or snap in annoyance? Or simply acknowledge that we all miss things sometimes, and move on together? The inconvenience is real—my pride, perhaps not so much.

If my daughter doesn't respond to my advice right away, should I take it as defiance? Or trust that she's processing it in her own time? My intention to guide is real—my need to control the outcome, perhaps not so much.

If a colleague misses a deadline, should I lash out to prove a point? Or understand what held them back and work together to find a solution? The delay is real—my need to assert blame, perhaps not so much.

If my boss doesn't recognize my contribution, should I sulk in silence? Or should I speak my truth, reset, and keep moving forward?

If someone cuts me off in traffic, do I let it hijack my mood for the rest of the day? Or do I take a deep breath and keep my eyes on the road ahead—both literally and metaphorically?

If a waiter mixes up my order, should I scold him? Or choose kindness over conflict? It's not about the food— it's about who I choose to be at that moment.

These aren't just stories—they're gentle nudges to remind us that inner peace is a choice, not a privilege. And ultimately, my happiness is my responsibility. Not my spouse's. Not my boss's. Not society's.

This lens—of clarity, balance, and accountability—has guided me not only in my personal life but also in the professional space.

That's where this book comes in.

Building on the foundation of happiness and self-awareness, **Touching the Core** moves the conversation into the heart of leadership. In today's dynamic and uncertain world, leadership is no longer about wielding authority—it's about inspiring trust. It's not about knowing all the answers but about asking the questions that matter. Over the years, I've learned—from mentors, teammates, books, and life itself—that the best leaders don't demand respect; they earn it, one action at a time.

This book isn't built on a single definition of leadership. Instead, it explores multiple dimensions that shape a complete leader—courage, humility, gratitude, authenticity, resilience, and service. Woven together through real stories, personal reflections, and hard-earned lessons from the front lines, it offers a roadmap to lead with clarity and purpose. Because just like happiness, leadership is a practice—one rooted in perspective, presence, and the pursuit of self-mastery.

Yes, I am familiar with the respected leadership theories and management frameworks created by experts around the world. These models provide valuable structure and insight, helping us navigate the complexities of organizations and teams. But this book dares to go beyond the blueprint. It steps into the lived experience of leadership—the kind that reveals itself not in boardrooms or PowerPoint slides, but in hallway conversations, crisis calls at midnight, and moments of quiet resolve. This is leadership defined by presence, not title. Rooted in simplicity, not complexity. Focused on action, not words.

It is about nurturing a leadership style that blends empathy with effectiveness, ambition with authenticity. It's about building cultures where people don't merely survive—they thrive. Where metrics serve meaning. Where success never comes at the expense of soul.

You'll find stories here that reflect what it truly means to lead. Stories of rolling up my sleeves—literally—after fifteen years away from the lab to stand beside my team when they needed support. Moments of choosing humility over hierarchy, connection over control. You'll meet leaders who serve more than they instruct, who empower more than they direct.

This is not a step-by-step manual. You won't find a rigid formula. But if you're seeking a path to lead from the inside out—to grow leadership that's as human as it is high-performing—then these pages are for you.

Whether you lead a team, nurture a family, mentor students, or simply strive for more meaning in your everyday actions, I invite you to walk with me.

Not just to lead others—but to truly, deeply lead yourself.

01

No Two Journeys Are the Same

Embracing Individual Backgrounds, Challenges, and Perspectives

Leadership begins with understanding—not just strategies and outcomes, but the very people we work with. Behind every task completed, every email sent, and every voice in a meeting is a journey shaped by experiences we may never fully know. And yet, leadership demands that we try to understand those journeys—not to judge, but to support, enable, and grow together.

As we know no two lives follow the same pattern. Some carry invisible burdens, while others have quietly fought battles no one saw. The same principle applies at the workplace. If we want to lead people meaningfully, we must recognize the individuality of their paths.

Understanding the Why Behind the Urgency

Let me share a story with you—one that shifted my perspective in ways I hadn't expected.

There was this colleague of mine who always seemed to be running around, sounding the alarm about every little thing. It was as though everything he did was an "emergency" that had to be escalated. The moment I saw his name pop up on my inbox, I'd brace myself for yet another urgent request. At first, I dismissed it—after all, how could so many things be that urgent all the time? It felt a bit like the boy who cried wolf. I found it irritating and decided to ignore his constant hustle, especially when it involved me. "He's just overreacting," I'd think.

But then, one day, we both happened to be at the coffee corner—two people caught in that brief, fleeting moment when you're not in work mode but in the realm of real conversation. I decided to ask him. I said, *"Hey, I've noticed you escalate everything like it's a crisis. Why is that?"*

To my surprise, he didn't get defensive. Instead, he gave me a candid look and said, *"Honestly, I don't like doing it. It frustrates me too. But here's the thing—I've got to prove to my manager that I'm always on top of things. If I don't make it seem urgent, I feel invisible. I don't think my work will be noticed otherwise."*

That conversation hit me like a ton of bricks. Suddenly, what I had written off as "drama" wasn't just noise—it was a survival mechanism. He wasn't looking for attention; he was desperately trying to make sure his efforts didn't go unnoticed. He was trapped in a cycle, trying to prove his worth in an environment that fostered micromanagement and deep-seated distrust.

It made me realize how much of what we see in others can be a result of external pressures, not personal shortcomings. From that day on, I made an effort to acknowledge his work. During my presentations to senior management, I highlighted his contributions, even the small ones. The change was remarkable. Slowly, his anxiety lessened. The urgency that used to follow him like a shadow started to fade. And most importantly, he began to trust that his work was being seen—not because he was shouting for attention, but because I recognized it.

That moment was a powerful reminder that sometimes, the behaviour we label as annoying or unnecessary is simply a sign of someone trying to navigate their own challenges in a way that makes them feel valued. It was an opportunity to shift from judgment to understanding. And as a leader, that's the kind of shift that can change everything.

From Mismatch to Masterpiece

Sometimes, we don't choose who we work with—but fate has a way of placing the right people in our paths, even if the reasons aren't immediately obvious.

I happened to work with a colleague who, from the very beginning, struck me as one of the most genuine souls I'd met in a professional setting. She was soft-spoken, unfailingly polite, and carried herself with quiet sincerity. There was a calm decency about her that instantly earned respect. And yet—despite her best intentions—her performance never quite matched her presence.

Execution was her Achilles' heel. Instructions had to be repeated. Deliverables came in half-baked. Feedback felt like it evaporated. I did everything I could as her manager—guided her patiently, explained things in simpler terms, gave her space to grow. But it was like pouring water into a pot with a tiny leak; something essential just wasn't holding.

At times, I found myself puzzled. Why wasn't this clicking? She was clearly trying—but the outcomes remained patchy. She rarely reached out to me proactively, and when she did, it was often after things had gone sideways. There was effort, no doubt. But there was also a visible disconnect between intention and impact.

It wasn't until a discussion with HR that the fog began to lift. As it turned out, she had landed in this department not by design, but by accident—a shuffle of internal movements had placed her in a highly technical role for which she had no foundational background. No wonder she was floundering— she was navigating unfamiliar terrain with no map.

That moment shifted everything for me.

She wasn't incompetent—she was miscast. She wasn't unwilling—she was misaligned.

I stopped focusing on what wasn't working and started asking: what could work? I sat down with her, not as a manager, but as a curious observer. What unfolded was a revelation. Beneath the quiet demeanour was a creative thinker with a brilliant eye for storytelling. She had an innate ability to connect dots, design narratives, and bring ideas to life visually. It was as if we had been trying to use a paintbrush to hammer a nail. The tool wasn't wrong—we were just using it in the wrong way.

So, I recalibrated. I began involving her in tasks that leaned into her strengths—creative campaigns, visual concepts, internal communications, and presentations. And just like that, the same individual who had once struggled to deliver now began to thrive. Her contributions came alive with flair and freshness. She wasn't just executing—she was owning her work, radiating purpose and confidence.

It was a transformation that not only benefitted her but reshaped how I viewed team dynamics altogether. Her journey became a benchmark for how we realigned talent across roles. We eventually supported her transition into a new space that fit her like a glove.

She reminded me that behind every struggling performer, there could be an uncut gem waiting to shine—if only someone paused long enough to notice the glint beneath the dust. Leadership is not about fixing people. It's about discovering them. And sometimes, what looks like a mismatch is a masterpiece waiting for its canvas.

As leaders, our role is not to judge behaviour at face value but to be curious about its roots. When we take the time to ask *"why,"* we can unlock understanding, dissolve tension, and rebuild trust.

In today's workplace, filled with diversity of culture, thought, and upbringing, leaders must be more than task-drivers. They must be bridge-builders—connecting individual stories with collective goals. They must create environments where people feel safe being themselves and supported in their growth.

Understanding backgrounds and challenges is not a soft skill—it's a strategic one. It reduces friction, builds morale, and unlocks creativity. It reminds us that people perform best when they are seen, heard, and valued—not just managed.

Leadership begins not with knowing the way, but with knowing the people who are walking it with you.

Key Takeaways:

- Every individual brings a unique journey to the workplace. Their behaviour, responses, and work styles are shaped by experiences we may not see—leaders must learn to see beyond the surface.
- Judgment creates distance; curiosity builds connection. When we seek to understand rather than react, we foster empathy and trust.
- Micromanagement and lack of acknowledgment can distort behaviour. Sometimes, people shout just to be heard. Leaders must create environments where visibility does not require raised volume.

Reflections:

- Think of a colleague or team member who has consistently challenged your patience or expectations. Could there be unseen circumstances or hidden strengths influencing their behaviour?

- Have you ever been in a situation where your potential was misunderstood or misaligned with your role? What helped you overcome it—or what could have helped?

- As a leader, do you make space to understand where someone is coming from before deciding where they should go?

- Are there talents in your team that might be underutilized simply because they don't fit the conventional Mold?

"Leadership is not about molding people into a standard shape. It's about discovering the unique light in each person and helping it shine."

– Unknown

02

Unearth the Best in Yourself and Others

Leadership begins with self-awareness and faith in human potential.

The foundation of great leadership lies in self-awareness—understanding one's strengths and consciously using them to uplift others. Too often, leadership is mistaken for authority and control, but true leaders don't impose change—they inspire it. They recognize their own capabilities and intentionally cultivate the potential in those around them. It all begins with a genuine belief in people and the power of human growth.

Someone once said, "*The world resides between our ears*" and the greatest discovery we can make is self-discovery. There is no deeper wisdom than truly understanding yourself—who you are, why you're here, what you can achieve, and how you can impact the world. When you embrace this, confidence grows. You begin to meet challenges not with fear, but with clarity and purpose.

Seeing the Whole Chessboard

In every new role I have taken, the rulebook came with crisp clarity—tasks to complete, targets to chase, and timelines etched in stone. But somewhere between doing what I was told and observing how everything connected, I realized I wasn't wired to play only my piece on the board. I needed to see the whole chessboard.

This instinct—to step back and understand not just the "*what*", but the "*why*" and the "*what if*"—grew stronger with every passing day. I wasn't just curious; I was compelled to explore the broader canvas. Soon, I found myself explaining projects not just in technical terms, but in ways that made people sit up and say, "*Now I see why this matters.*"

What began as personal curiosity slowly transformed into a leadership compass. I began connecting dots others didn't even realize existed—highlighting overlooked risks, unrealized value, and new pathways of impact. And as I shared those insights, something remarkable happened: people around me started thinking bigger, too. Teams grew more aligned, more aware. The questions became sharper. The outcomes, stronger.

I recall one particular project soon after I joined a new organization. It came down from the top— a high-priority initiative directly advised by the business head. The setup was swift: roles were handed out, budgets allocated, timelines set. The energy was electric—everyone wanted to execute and deliver. But amidst all that movement, no one seemed to be asking: *Why are we doing this? What's the end game? Are we prepared for what lies beneath the surface?*

I stayed quiet initially, not wanting to be "that new guy" who slows things down. But I couldn't ignore my gut. Quietly, in parallel, I began building the wider context—digging into the market dynamics, analysing the ecosystem, scrutinizing internal capabilities. After a few days, I presented my findings. What followed was silence. Then, interest. Then, action. Timelines were adjusted, assumptions challenged, and additional budgets sanctioned. It wasn't just about the information—it was about a mindset shift: from racing ahead to moving forward wisely.

Another time, we had a product that looked great on the outside—solid market price, decent acceptance. But something didn't add up. I sensed the discomfort of the manufacturing team—the furrowed brows, the reluctant nods. So, I dug deeper. What I found was a ticking time bomb: operational inefficiencies bleeding profitability, masked by the illusion of market performance. It would've been easier to ride the wave. Instead, I chose to challenge the tide.

Armed with data, I made the case for discontinuation—a bold move, but the right one. It wasn't a popular decision. But it saved the company time, money, and future headaches. More importantly, it reinforced the principle I've come to live by: Leadership is not about having all the answers—it's about having the courage to ask the deeper questions.

These experiences taught me a vital truth: when you develop self-awareness and choose to look beyond your lane, you don't just elevate your own performance—you lift the entire team. You spark clarity. You awaken confidence. You inspire growth.

That is what unearthing the best in ourselves and others really means: seeing beyond the task to the transformation. Helping people zoom out so they can zoom in with sharper focus. And cultivating a culture where the big picture isn't just seen—it's shared.

See the Spark, Not the Flaws

I once had a team member whose written communication skills were, quite honestly, abysmal. Emails lacked clarity, reports were riddled with errors, and even simple summaries fell short of expectations. I tried everything—constructive feedback, coaching sessions, writing tips—but the improvement was marginal at best. My frustration grew.

But then, something nudged me to look beyond the obvious.

This same individual had an extraordinary ability to grasp complex instructions in a flash. He could detect loopholes and inconsistencies others glossed over. His root cause analyses were sharp, practical, and grounded. He was a natural collaborator, able to pull the right people together and engineer solutions efficiently.

And so, I asked myself: *If someone brings such immense value to the table, why am I spending so much energy trying to fix what may not be their zone of genius?*

That question became a turning point. I stopped pushing him to improve his writing and instead began leveraging his strengths. I took on the responsibility for the written work where needed, freeing him to focus on problem-solving and execution—where he truly excelled.

What followed was nothing short of transformation. His productivity surged. His confidence bloomed. And, to my surprise, his writing began to improve on its own. Not because of more feedback—but because he no longer felt judged. He felt trusted and empowered resulting in more conviction and clarity.

That experience taught me a profound lesson: Leadership isn't about ironing out every wrinkle. It's about recognizing brilliance—even if it comes in an unconventional package—and nurturing it. When we stop trying to "fix" people and instead start believing in them, they often end up growing in ways we never imagined.

A Dusty Letter, A Lasting Lesson

It was just another ordinary afternoon—or so I thought. I was clearing the clutter from my desk, the kind of task you keep postponing until it starts whispering your name louder than your to-do list. As I moved aside a stubborn stack of long-forgotten files, something slipped loose and fluttered to the floor.

A folded piece of paper, yellowed slightly with time and edged in dust.

Instinctively, I almost tossed it into the bin. But something about its weight—or perhaps its silence—stopped me. I opened it. And in that moment, the world grew still.

It was a handwritten note. A thank-you letter. From an intern who had spent only a couple of fleeting months with us, years ago.

In this age of pings, likes, and two-second replies, the curves and slants of his inked handwriting felt intimate, almost sacred. Line by line, his words reached across time and touched something deep within me.

He wrote of the guidance I'd offered, the way I had broken down complex ideas until they felt simple, even exciting. He remembered being entrusted with work that mattered, being listened to, being seen—not just as an intern, but as a person trying to find his place in the world.

What moved me most wasn't the praise. It was the realization that what I considered routine—explaining a task patiently, inviting him into a conversation, letting him try and fail safely—had meant the world to him. Those moments had lingered in his memory long after he left. And now, years later, they had come back to me in his words.

As I finished reading, a quiet, humbling truth settled in my heart: We rarely know the full reach of our actions.

We tend to measure leadership in outcomes, strategies, performance charts. But this letter reminded me that real leadership often lives in the invisible moments—the ones where we pause to guide, to believe in someone, to offer just a little more of ourselves than necessary.

That dusty note didn't just remind me of a young intern's journey. It reminded me of my own. Of why I choose to lead the way I do. Not to command, but to nurture. Not to impress, but to invest.

Because when we lift others, we don't just shape their path—we discover the deeper purpose behind our own. And sometimes, the most profound lessons come not from books or boardrooms, but from a forgotten letter waiting patiently to be found.

Uplift the Gifted, Empower the Growing

One of the foundational truths I've come to believe is this: talent is not a trophy—it's a responsibility. Being gifted isn't something to boast about; it's something to be grateful for. Talent—whether in the form of intelligence, creativity, empathy, or technical prowess—is a gift, often shaped by unseen advantages: a good mentor, early exposure, access to resources, or simply the right environment.

And because not everyone starts from the same line, those of us who've had the chance to grow must also make room for others to rise. Real leadership lies not just in maximizing talent, but in redistributing opportunity. It means being just as invested in the progress of the struggling as in the success of the shining stars.

This idea of balancing excellence with inclusivity came alive in a memorable interview I once came across for a senior leadership position. The question was deceptively simple, but my response revealed profound wisdom.

Interviewer: *How would you increase the productivity of a low performer in your team?*

Me: (After a pause) *While there may be a low performer, I'm sure there's also a high performer. I'd begin by enhancing the high performer's productivity.*

Interviewer: (Interrupting) *Do you mean to deprive the low performer of guidance or support?*

Me: (With calm clarity) *Not at all. I would devote 70% of my energy to the high performer—to sustain momentum—and 30% to the low performer—to listen, encourage, and guide. Productivity is ultimately self-driven. Everyone has potential, but it must be matched by intent. By nurturing high performers, we create a dynamic environment that others naturally aspire to. It's also the right time to challenge them with bigger goals—sparking a ripple effect of excellence.*

Interviewer: *But why focus on someone already doing well?*

Me: *Because we often assume they don't need us. But even the best seed won't grow in dry soil. High performers thrive on appreciation, direction, and challenge. When we nourish them, we set new standards that elevate the whole team.*

That answer has stayed with me ever since. It captured a principle I've held close throughout my journey: never overlook the flourishing for the struggling and never neglect the struggling while nurturing the flourishing. Both need your presence—just in different ways.

Key Takeaways:

- Leadership starts with self-awareness. Knowing your strengths is the first step to helping others grow.
- Talent is a responsibility. Use your gifts to uplift others—not to set yourself apart.
- See the whole chessboard. Step back, connect the dots, and lead with broader insight.
- Lead with courageous curiosity. Ask deeper questions—even when it's uncomfortable.
- Build on strengths. Focus on what people do well, not just where they fall short.
- Support both the strong and the struggling. High performers need nurturing too; growth happens at all levels.

Reflections:

- What strength of yours can you use to help someone else grow?
- Are you giving enough attention to both your top talent and your hidden ones?
- Where can you zoom out to gain better clarity—and help others do the same?

"The task of leadership is not to put greatness into people, but to elicit it, for the greatness is there already."

– John Buchan

03

Eyes Are Always on You

How your behavior silently sets the tone for
your team.

Leadership often evokes images of bold decisions, commanding presence, and charismatic influence. But some of the most profound leadership happens in silence—through consistency, self-awareness, and behavior that others naturally observe and mirror.

The Quiet Power of Showing Up

During my PhD, writing was nothing more than a box to tick—another academic requirement. But something unexpected happened. What started as a task gradually turned into a calling. I began to enjoy the process of taking tangled thoughts and weaving them into clear, meaningful narratives. With each published article, I discovered not just the thrill of contribution, but the quiet joy of clarity. My words were reaching corners of the world I'd never seen, and in return, I was learning to think more sharply, more deeply.

That small spark became a steady flame. Long after my academic days, I kept writing—sometimes technical pieces, sometimes personal reflections. It evolved from a task to a ritual, from performance to practice. I never spoke much about it, never turned it into a campaign. I just wrote—because it helped me understand myself and the world better.

What started as a passion has now evolved into discipline. Writing is no longer something I wait to feel inspired to do—it is a practice I show up for, like a daily ritual. Even on the days when the words don't come easily, I write. Because I've come to realize writing isn't just how I express myself—it's how I understand myself. It sharpens my thinking, slows down my assumptions, and turns noise into meaning. It has become my quiet form of leadership.

Years later, a colleague approached me with a quiet smile. *"I've been reading your posts,"* she said. *"I've never written anything before, but I'd like to try. You've inspired me."* She set a goal to write her first article. I offered encouragement and a few tips, but the drive was all hers. And when her article finally went live, the shift in her was undeniable. Her ideas became clearer, her communication more confident, her impact more visible.

That moment reminded me of something profound:

People don't always need loud leaders. Sometimes, they just need someone who shows up consistently.

We often underestimate the influence of steady, silent effort. But others are watching—not to evaluate, but to emulate. And often, the most powerful inspiration isn't a rousing speech, but a quiet example repeated over time. You don't need to shout to lead. Sometimes, writing quietly in a corner, week after week, speaks louder than any podium ever could.

Lead Yourself First

Leadership isn't always about leading others. It begins with leading ourselves—with composure, conviction, and purpose. It's about managing our own reactions, staying grounded amid chaos, and resisting the urge to prove ourselves constantly to people who may not even be equipped to evaluate our worth.

Take, for example, a time early in my career when I was bypassed for a promotion I had clearly earned. While disappointment bubbled inside me, I made a conscious decision not to let it show in my performance or my interactions. Instead, I doubled down on my work, refined my skills, and supported my team even more strongly. A few months later, a bigger opportunity came along—one I might have missed had I let frustration derail me. Leadership begins with this kind of inner steadiness.

From Validation to Alignment

Don't get caught up in the race to prove yourself—especially when those around you might not even be qualified to appreciate your worth. Instead, focus on believing in yourself and consistently doing what aligns with your values and benefits the people around you. Let your actions and results speak so clearly that they can't be ignored, even by those you once sought validation from.

A colleague of mine, an incredibly competent analyst, was often overlooked because he wasn't loud about his achievements. But over time, his insights began driving major decisions, and even the most sceptical leaders began turning to him for input. He never had to raise his voice. His impact did the talking.

Power, Used Wisely

This principle is liberating. It shifts your focus from external approval to internal alignment. It helps you model integrity and resilience—the qualities your team will naturally begin to mirror.

In the workplace, the freedom that comes with authority is a double-edged sword. Some use it to evolve and empower others, while some drift into complacency. But the way we use our freedom—and how we carry our power—shapes how others perceive us and behave around us. If you want a culture of ownership, growth, and discipline, model it yourself.

I recall a senior leader who always arrived on time for every meeting, even when he was the most senior person in the room. Without a single word, he set a tone for discipline and respect that trickled down through the ranks. That's the power of modelled leadership.

Respond, Don't React

As a leader, it's crucial to remember that there is always a solution to every problem. What matters most is the approach and tools we use to find that solution. Whether we choose stress, impatience, frustration, anger—or their opposites— will define our character, influence our team's well-being, and shape the culture of our organization.

Every challenge is an opportunity not just to solve but to demonstrate—through calm, focus, and positivity—that leadership is about steadiness, not just strategy.

We were just weeks away from a major product launch when things started to unravel. The issue? We couldn't match the expected product quality despite all our efforts. Timelines slipped, and the pressure became unbearable. The sales team was up in arms rightly worried about losing market momentum. Tensions soared, and soon, panic began to ripple across the organization.

As the project in-charge, I understood exactly how serious the problem was—but I also knew the issues weren't due to negligence. They were the result of complex, unforeseen technical challenges. Escalating the panic wouldn't solve anything.

So instead of joining the noise, I did the opposite—I called for calm.

I brought all the stakeholders together and laid the facts bare. No sugarcoating, no excuses—just clarity. I acknowledged the quality gaps, shared the root causes, and presented realistic paths forward. Then I did something even more important: I listened. And that made all the difference.

The room shifted from blame to problem-solving. Frustration gave way to focus. The calmness became contagious. Together, we made tough but necessary calls, reworked timelines, and pulled in extra support where it mattered most.

In the end, we didn't just recover—we emerged stronger. The product launch still happened, slightly delayed but with uncompromised quality. More importantly, we turned a crisis into a catalyst. The trust, cohesion, and confidence we built in that moment went far beyond one project.

The Inner Landscape of Leadership

It's equally important to manage our inner world. Controlling impulsive behaviour despite stress, staying patient in the face of pressure, and choosing empathy when frustrated—these aren't just signs of maturity; they are hallmarks of leadership.

Your ability to listen to others even when you are burdened yourself reflects the depth of your character.

Think of the leader who, despite a family emergency, still makes time to coach a struggling team member—because they understand the ripple effect of presence and compassion. Such gestures linger far longer in people's memories than grand speeches or performance metrics.

Stay Humble, Keep Growing

True leaders understand that growth is continuous. And with growth comes the wisdom to unlearn, to stay curious, and to embrace change without ego. Many people have ideas on how others should change; few have ideas on how they should change.

Recognizing your own growth gives you confidence—but staying humble ensures that growth never stops.

I once worked with a VP who attended a junior team's brainstorming session, not to supervise, but to learn. He openly said, *"You're closer to the problem than I am—I'm here to listen."* That humility earned him respect that no job title ever could.

Let Your Presence Speak

So, when you reach a stage where you deliver value without needing validation, where your energy uplifts others, and where your behaviour quietly sets standards without needing to speak—you've truly stepped into leadership. Be the example. Let your presence do the talking. That's real leadership.

Key Takeaways:

- Leadership is not just spoken—it is demonstrated through everyday behaviour.
- People are always watching, consciously or unconsciously modelling your actions.
- Leading yourself with integrity, calm, and self-discipline sets a powerful tone for your team.
- Don't waste energy proving yourself to people who may not understand your value—focus on aligning with your values and contributing meaningfully.

- Use your freedom and power wisely—they can elevate or erode trust depending on how they're used.
- Emotional regulation during stress is not just maturity—it's contagious leadership.
- Every problem has a solution—your attitude in solving it defines your culture.
- Consistent habits (like writing, reflection, learning) silently inspire others to follow.

Reflections:

- Are your daily actions aligned with the values you want your team to adopt?
- In what ways might you be unintentionally influencing your team—for better or worse?
- What personal habit or trait do you model today that someone else may silently be learning from?

"The most powerful leadership tool you have is your own personal example."

– John Wooden

04

Give Generously—Especially Appreciation

The Power of Recognition in Building
Trust and Motivation

Appreciation is one of the most underestimated yet powerful tools a leader, parent, or peer can use. It doesn't cost anything, but its return is immeasurable. In both professional and personal contexts, recognition has the power to boost morale, deepen trust, and drive individuals to outperform even their own expectations. I understood this more deeply—not in a boardroom, but in the backseat conversations with my daughters during school pickups.

How Recognition Shapes Motivation

During my work-from-home days, I often carve out time to pick them up from school. These drives home have become moments of unexpected insight. Sometimes, they can't stop talking—sharing every detail about their day, their lessons, their teachers, and friends. Other times, I sense that something's off. They're quiet or visibly upset. As I try to piece together their stories while driving, I occasionally lose track or miss the context, which annoys them. Still, I make it a point to stay engaged and ask questions.

Over time, I noticed something interesting. They spoke about teachers with strong opinions—clearly favouring some over others. But when I tried to understand the reasons behind these preferences, it wasn't the difficulty of the subject or teaching style that stood out. It was appreciation. The teachers who gave verbal praise, wrote positive notes in their diaries, or rewarded them with a star stamp on the hand were always in their "good books." The ones who didn't? Often disregarded or even disliked.

But it didn't stop at the teachers. The girls started associating entire subjects with how much appreciation they received. If a math teacher didn't show encouragement, suddenly math was "boring" or "difficult." But if an English teacher celebrated their writing, English quickly became their favourite subject. They began actively engaging with content that they knew would bring appreciation.

Does that sound familiar?

Lack of appreciation isn't just a fleeting moment—it can cascade into how people feel about their work, their environment, and even themselves. This lesson, as I observed it through my children, is profoundly true in the workplace too.

Appreciation in the Workplace: More Than a Gesture

Let's face it—adults aren't that different from kids. We may wear suits and carry titles, but deep down, we still light up when someone notices our effort. Recognition isn't childish—it's human. And in the workplace, it's not just a perk. It's fuel.

Teams don't run only on salary slips and performance reviews. They run on trust, belonging, and the simple magic of being appreciated. Yet how often do we pause to say, "*Well done*," not just for big wins, but for the quiet grind—the extra effort, the late nights, the invisible lifts?

I've seen it with my own eyes: appreciation doesn't just motivate individuals—it transforms teams. It builds bridges across departments, melts away silos, and replaces quiet resentment with shared pride. And the best part? It costs nothing but delivers returns we can't even measure.

Thankfully, the corporate world is catching on. More and more organizations are waking up to this powerful truth: appreciation drives performance. Not hypothetically. Tangibly. Strategically. It's no longer an optional "feel-good" activity—it's becoming a structured part of business growth.

Today, you'll find intentional interventions—quarterly appreciation rituals, recognition walls, peer shout-outs, team celebrations after milestones. I've been part of sessions where team members openly thank each other, not just for project wins, but for support, empathy, and that one time someone stayed late to help out.

And the impact? Electric. People walk out of those rooms taller, prouder, more connected. Productivity rises, attrition drops, and the energy shift is unmistakable. When people feel valued, they don't just do their jobs—they show up with heart.

In a world chasing speed and scale, don't underestimate the quiet power of a heartfelt *"thank you."* A single word can change someone's day. A culture of appreciation! It can change everything.

The Deeper Power of Appreciation

Let's be clear—appreciation isn't the same as praise. Praise can be polite. Appreciation is personal. It says: *I see you. I value what you did. And it mattered.* It's not just feel-good fluff—it's fuel for growth.

Think of it like this: a plant can survive on sunlight and water, but it thrives when you add the right nutrients. People are the same. Sure, they'll show up for the pay check. But when you add recognition into the mix—genuine, timely, specific appreciation—they come alive. They go beyond the call of duty not because they must, but because they want to.

And it doesn't always take grand gestures. Sometimes a leader's silent nod, a handwritten note, or a simple *"I noticed what you did—thank you"* can light someone up for days. That's the secret power of meaningful appreciation: it acknowledges not just the output, but the effort behind it. It touches people's dignity.

I experienced this firsthand during a particularly demanding project. One of my colleagues had quietly gone above and beyond to solve a last-minute challenge that could've delayed the entire launch. While most of the credit could have easily gone to the front-facing team, I made it a point to personally acknowledge his contribution in front of the leadership team—

citing exactly what he had done and why it mattered. Later, he told me it was the first time in his career he felt "truly seen." That simple act not only boosted his morale but also sparked a visible shift in his confidence and ownership moving forward.

But here's the catch—appreciation must be authentic. Spray-and-pray compliments won't cut it. I once watched a manager publicly applaud everyone, everywhere, all the time—"*Great job! Fantastic work! Brilliant idea!*" At first, it was energizing. But soon, people tuned out. Why? Because it wasn't backed by specifics or sincerity. Quiet contributors felt invisible. Overlooked. And what started as motivation ended up as noise.

Appreciation should never be used carelessly or performatively. It's not a PR tool—it's a leadership tool. Just like feedback, advice, or coaching, it must be wielded thoughtfully. Impartially. Intentionally. Done right, it doesn't just lift morale—it deepens trust, builds loyalty, and brings out the best in people.

People don't just want to be noticed—they want to be understood. A culture of real appreciation turns workplaces from transactional to transformational. Because when people feel seen, they show up—not just with their hands, but with their hearts.

Self-Motivation and Maturity in Leadership

At the same time, it's important to understand that seeking appreciation obsessively can be counterproductive. Craving external validation is a sign of emotional dependence.

Leaders—true leaders—are driven by a deep sense of purpose and inner clarity. They don't perform to be praised; they perform because it's the right thing to do.

Once you transcend the need for applause as your primary motivator, you've already reached a major milestone in leadership. Recognition will come—maybe quietly, maybe later—but it will come, and it will be well-earned.

It Also Makes You Happier

Appreciating others doesn't just benefit them—it enriches you as well. Watching someone's face light up in response to your words or gestures brings an undeniable sense of satisfaction, gratitude, and joy. It's one of those rare moments when giving feels as fulfilling as receiving.

I'll never forget a moment when I sent a simple message to my editor from an external agency, acknowledging how her behind-the-scenes efforts had added a valuable dimension to my article. It wasn't something I was required to do—I just genuinely felt impressed by the quality of her work and wanted to let her know. Her reply? "*You just made my week.*" That small gesture of appreciation made my day. It was a reminder of how powerful even the simplest acts of gratitude can be—for both the giver and the receiver.

Key Takeaways:

- Appreciation isn't optional—it's essential. It fuels motivation, fosters trust, and shapes long-term engagement.

- It must flow in all directions. Managers need appreciation as much as team members do. Appreciation should be mutual, not hierarchical.

- Silence can speak louder than words. Non-verbal cues of recognition—when genuine—can have a lasting emotional impact.

- Beware of biases. Appreciation must be fair, timely, and inclusive. Unequal praise can be damaging.

- Don't depend on applause. The strongest leaders perform for purpose, not for praise.

- Appreciation is fertilizer. Without it, people may survive; with it, they flourish.

- Appreciating others brings joy. Seeing the effect of your recognition on others is a reward in itself.

Reflections:

- When was the last time you genuinely appreciated someone's effort at work or home?

- Do you wait for grand successes to give appreciation, or do you celebrate small wins too?

- How do you respond when you don't receive appreciation? Could you reframe your expectations to find fulfilment in your actions instead?

- Is there someone you've taken for granted lately? What's stopping you from telling them they're valued—today?

"Appreciation is not praise—it's presence. It's the quiet recognition that someone's effort mattered."

– From the Author

05

Zoom Out: See the Bigger Picture

Why perspective matters more than control.

Leadership is not always about doing more—it's often about thinking differently. As we grow in our careers, the nature of our contributions must evolve. There comes a time when growth is no longer about task execution alone—it becomes about strategic thinking, vision, and seeing beyond the immediate. Strategic thinking enables us to craft a vision and pave the way for growth, not just for ourselves but for our teams and our entire organization. Task execution might deliver immediate results, but without the guidance of strategic perspective, it risks being shortsighted and unsustainable.

Shift the Lens, Unlock the Potential

During one phase of my career, I had the opportunity to serve as a Sales Leader for a short stint at an organization that was once a domestic player but had recently been acquired by a global multinational. My role, coming from the parent multinational company, was to support cultural integration and drive sales growth in alignment with global expectations.

On the surface, everything appeared to be progressing well—the infrastructure was upgraded, quality systems were in place and revenue numbers were on track. However, when I started connecting with individual members of my team, I noticed something missing beneath the surface: a lack of motivation.

Despite introducing exciting strategies and offering hands-on support, I sensed that my efforts weren't landing. The team appeared agreeable and nodded in meetings, but there was no genuine initiative or drive to implement the ideas. It took almost two months of deeper conversations and observations to uncover the real issue—a crisis of self-identity.

The sales managers, though loyal and capable, had been assigned roles more by organizational convenience than by personal strengths. Responsibilities were handed out based on client connections or immediate availability, not by aligning with individuals' domain expertise. As a result, the team lacked ownership and clarity in their roles—everyone was simply titled "Sales Manager," with no clear purpose beyond transactional execution.

This insight shifted my focus. Rather than fixating on control or sales KPIs, I decided to zoom out and see the bigger picture—the root cause of disengagement was structural, not strategic. I held one-on-one sessions with key team members and discovered that many had deep knowledge of specific sectors—some specialized in pharmaceuticals, others in agriculture, and a few had strong roots in oil and refinery segments.

That became the seed for a new approach. I proposed restructuring the organogram based on industry verticals. Instead of being generalist sales managers, they would now become "Industry Leads" or "Category Experts," each responsible for driving strategy, ownership, and outcomes in their respective domains. It took effort and buy-in from multiple stakeholders as it involved restructuring customer accountability. However, once approved and implemented, the transformation was remarkable.

This redefined structure gave people not just job titles—but identity, ownership, and pride in their roles. Their energy shifted, collaboration improved, and results followed. Had I stayed fixated on enforcing sales targets or micromanaging execution, this outcome would have never emerged. But by stepping back and taking a broader view, we unlocked something far more powerful than numbers—we unlocked potential.

This small but meaningful shift created waves. Motivation soared, collaboration improved, and ownership became real. I didn't just unlock performance—I unlocked purpose. Years later, those same colleagues still express how that moment transformed their career trajectories. That's the power of perspective.

Plan Ahead While the Present Is Strong

The best time to plan for the future is when your present is stable. Stability brings clarity and space to think ahead. When we're in crisis mode, our vision shrinks to the next urgent decision. But when we're doing well, we have the opportunity to be proactive rather than reactive. Let's use that moment of strength not just to celebrate, but to shape what's next.

At one point in my career, I was leading a product team that had just delivered its best quarterly performance. The mood was celebratory, and rightly so. But instead of simply riding the wave, I called for a strategic discussion—not to applaud our success, but to explore what could go wrong next. The team was puzzled. "*Why now?*" someone asked. My response: *Because now we have clarity, bandwidth, and confidence—the perfect soil to plant seeds of future resilience.*

During that session, we identified emerging threats from competitors—signals that hadn't yet disrupted us but had the potential to. We crafted alternative strategies and began building a parallel product basket to mitigate risk. Six months later, those very threats turned into a real challenge for the market—but not for us. We were ready. That moment of foresight transformed a potential crisis into a competitive edge which was also recognized by our customers.

The future belongs to those who prepare for it today.

Let's not just be managers. Let's be visionaries. Let's dare to zoom out.

Planting Trees, Not Just Picking Fruit

Often, organizations cling too tightly to instant ROI, linking every initiative to immediate financial outcomes. While financial performance is important, measuring only by short-term returns creates a dangerous blind spot. Promotional activities, market expansion, and capability-building initiatives may not yield instant results, but they are foundational to long-term value.

Organizations that prioritize only immediate outcomes:

- Undermine innovation and long-term thinking
- Discourage visionary, transformational roles
- Risk stalling sustainable growth

Instead, balance the financial KPIs with non-financial indicators like brand recall, market penetration, and customer sentiment. True vision lies in long-term planning and patience. To make this possible, every organization should establish a dedicated division for transformational initiatives—staffed with capable individuals who shape the future—while the rest of the organization focuses on sustaining and growing the core business. This transformational division should focus on areas such as digital innovation, new business models, sustainability initiatives, culture change, thought leadership, and human capability building. By insulating this unit from the pressures of short-term performance, organizations can create space for experimentation, agility, and bold thinking—elements essential for long-term leadership.

Key Takeaways:

- Strategic thinking elevates your contribution from transactional to transformational.
- Seeing the bigger picture helps uncover root causes that numbers alone can't show.

- Redesigning roles around identity and purpose can reignite motivation.
- Embrace change, even when it means letting go of familiar comfort.
- Long-term success requires balancing immediate ROI with future-focused investments.
- Use moments of stability to think ahead and plan proactively.
- Great leaders are not just efficient—they are insightful.

Reflections:

- Think of a recent situation where you were deeply focused on execution. What might you have seen differently if you had taken a step back to consider the bigger picture?
- What opportunities for growth—yours or your team's—are currently hidden behind short-term pressures?
- How can you create space for more strategic thinking in your day-to-day leadership?

"You can't see the whole picture while you're in the frame."

– Les Brown

06

People Crave Purpose, Not Just Pay checks

Fulfilment Comes from Meaning, Not Money

People don't just work for salaries—they work for significance. While financial compensation is essential, it rarely fuels long-term motivation. What truly energizes individuals is a sense of purpose: knowing that their work matters, that it contributes to something larger, and that their efforts are seen and valued.

Bridging the Gap—From Transaction to Transformation

I had the privilege of working in a globally respected organization—one that had scaled across continents not just in revenue, but in reputation, impact, and culture. It was a place where people proudly dedicated decades of their careers. That pride was infectious—and I felt a strong desire to contribute in a way that truly mattered.

So, I rolled up my sleeves and began connecting directly with sales teams across geographies. While the energy around targets was sky-high, I quickly noticed a missing link: purpose. The conversations were intensely goal-driven but shallow—more about discounts and volumes than about the value we brought to customers' lives and innovations. Most of the engagement happened with procurement—not the scientists or engineers who used our products.

This gap dulled innovation and dimmed excitement. Sales teams were great at how to sell but unclear on why it mattered. Technical challenges were treated like detours instead of drivers of value.

I knew we could do better. But I also knew I couldn't do it alone.

This was a massive shift to drive—and it needed scale, speed, and support. So, I turned inward and focused on empowering my own team. I mentored them, shared context, transferred knowledge, and brought them up to speed—not just technically, but strategically. We evolved from being a support function to becoming enablers of customer success.

Together, we created a new narrative. We crafted content that translated product features into real-world outcomes, tied solutions to specific customer pain points, and brought science to life through compelling use-case stories. We ran immersive training sessions, co-created customer presentations, and worked shoulder-to-shoulder with the sales teams until technical confidence turned into commercial courage.

And suddenly, things began to shift.

Sales conversations moved from price points to problem-solving. Team members began speaking not just at customers, but with them. Scientists were now part of the dialogue. Our teams started seeing themselves as enablers of innovation, not just executors of quotas.

It wasn't just about teaching product knowledge—it was about reigniting pride. It was about showing people their impact.

And the result? Sales teams didn't just become more effective—they became more fulfilled. Instead of retention efforts focused on keeping people in, we focused on unlocking what was already within them.

From Comfort Zone to Global Stage: How Purpose Ignited a Career

Early in my post-PhD corporate journey, I reached out to one of my juniors from college—a decent, hardworking, and bright young man I had always admired. At the time, he was working in a pharmaceutical company in his hometown—settled, secure, but stuck. When I offered him a role on my team, he was hesitant. "*It's a big leap,*" he said. "My current *job may not pay much, but it's safe.*" I could sense the fear of change pulling him back.

But I also saw untapped brilliance slowly fading in that comfort zone.

Convincing him to even consider the opportunity took time. But an even bigger challenge lay ahead—getting him through the interview. While technically sound, he struggled to articulate his thoughts and lacked confidence in his communication. I knew his potential, but the panel didn't.

So, I took a bold step—I spoke to the other interviewers, vouched for his capability, and requested they look beyond his presentation and trust the person behind it. They did. He was hired.

He joined—but the comfort of his past still clung to him. I could feel the tension in our daily conversations—he was physically present, but mentally unsure. That's when I realized: he didn't just need a job. He needed a reason to believe in himself again.

So, I helped him enrol in a PhD program, with me as his external guide. That one intervention flipped a switch. Within three years, he completed his research with astounding focus. But more than that, I watched him bloom. His confidence soared. His written communication became sharp and compelling. He started owning conversations with customers, asking insightful questions, and offering solutions.

He became one of the most dependable professionals in the team—not just technically, but as a complete package. Today, he's not in a lab coat. He's on airplanes, on global stages, building business for a multinational organization, and earning the trust of customers across the world.

The transformation? It didn't come from money. It came from meaning. From believing he could be more—and helping him see it too.

Purpose changed his trajectory. And that's a lesson every leader needs to remember: people don't just want pay checks—they want to matter.

Key Takeaways:

- Purpose drives performance—more than money ever can.
- Comfort zones limit growth; belief unlocks potential.
- Empowering teams creates lasting impact and ownership.
- Meaningful work transforms selling into storytelling.
- People stay where they feel valued—not just paid.

Reflections:

- How are you enabling the people around you to feel that their work matters?
- What can you do differently to help your team connect with the deeper purpose behind their everyday tasks?

"When people are financially invested, they want a return. When people are emotionally invested, they want to contribute."

– Simon Sinek

07

Bosses Command, Leaders Inspire

The Irony of Losing Leadership When We Chase Authority

There's an old saying: *"Power may open the door, but only trust will keep people in the room."*

Leadership based on authority can demand action—but it rarely earns respect. Command may bring temporary compliance, but inspiration fuels lasting transformation.

The more we chase authority for its own sake, the more we risk losing the essence of leadership. True leadership is earned, not imposed. It's not what you say from the top that defines your influence—it's what you stand for when nobody is watching. And when people believe in that vision, trust follows.

Let's look at the remarkable life of Shri Narendra Modi, one of the most transformational leaders of contemporary India, to explore what leadership really means.

Narendra Modi: From the Margins to the Mandate of Millions

Narendra Modi's rise isn't just inspiring—it's a living example of leadership born from purpose, not position. Born in 1950 in a small town in Gujarat, he had no political lineage, no wealth, no privilege—nothing that usually guarantees success. In fact, his early life was invisible to the power structures. But there was something different about him: he was observant, reflective, and unwaveringly determined.

What pushed him forward was not a hunger for power—it was his focus on development, public service, and a vision for India. Modi didn't demand followers—he earned them by offering a future people could believe in. His rise wasn't fuelled by title; it was built on authenticity, conviction, and a clear sense of purpose.

When Modi became the Chief Minister of Gujarat, his policies set off a revolution—infrastructure, economic growth, and good governance became the cornerstones of his tenure. His communication wasn't just about speaking—it was about making the people feel like they mattered. He made sure their voices were heard, and through this, his leadership gained momentum.

By the time he became Prime Minister of India in 2014, his success wasn't due to authority—it was the power of his vision. And vision is what wins hearts, not titles.

The Paradox of Power

Here's the irony: the more someone clings to authority, the less effective they are as leaders. Leadership isn't about controlling people—it's about empowering them. When people feel dictated to, they rebel. But when they feel included, when they feel trusted, they rise.

Modi's rise wasn't just about domestic policy—it was about reshaping India's role on the global stage. Under his leadership, India stopped being a satellite of superpowers and became a neutral force, standing tall as an independent power. He redefined India's foreign policy, ensuring that the country wasn't just a puppet to global powers but an active, neutral player in world affairs. He worked tirelessly to position India as a strategic partner, not just a passive actor.

His global strategy wasn't to side with one superpower or another; it was about fostering mutual respect and cooperation. Modi's foreign policy brought India out of its past, where it had often been dominated by the agendas of global powers. Instead, India became a respected voice, forging ties with countries across the world and building partnerships based on shared interests, innovation, and growth.

Inspiring Global Action Against Terrorism

One of Modi's most powerful contributions to global leadership was his ability to unite the world against one of the most pressing issues of our time: terrorism. Unlike many leaders who merely spoke about anti-terrorism, Modi actively brought countries together to combat terrorism in all forms.

He didn't just speak at the United Nations—he made sure the world listened. Under his leadership, India pushed for greater international cooperation on counterterrorism efforts, uniting nations that had once been divided on the issue. His stance wasn't just about diplomacy—it was about creating alliances that could unite against a global threat that knows no borders.

From the UN General Assembly to bilateral talks, Modi used every platform to forge a unified front against terrorism, driving home the point that this was a fight for the future of humanity, not just a fight for one nation. He galvanized the international community, pushing for actionable steps that extended beyond words and into coordinated actions.

Bosses Seek Control. Leaders Build Trust

Now, let's contrast Modi's leadership with those who rely on inherited power or climb through networks of privilege. Many of them, despite their titles, struggle to connect, inspire, and mobilize. Why? Because they rely on authority as a shortcut to influence. They issue orders, enforce compliance, and demand obedience, mistaking control for leadership.

But here's the truth: people don't follow titles. They follow leaders who make them feel seen, heard, and valued. They follow those who lead with conviction, purpose, and authenticity—not through fear, but through belief.

Modi didn't demand loyalty—he earned it. Whether addressing a village gathering or the United Nations, he led with clarity, conviction, and cultural authenticity. He didn't just speak; he mobilized people, turning national campaigns into personal missions for millions of citizens.

In a world full of bosses who cling to control, Modi's journey reminds us that true leadership isn't about authority—it's about inspiring action, building trust, and uniting people behind a cause greater than themselves.

Key Takeaways:

- Bosses may hold the mic, but leaders win hearts.
- Authority can fill a room, but only inspiration can move it.
- Leadership is not about commanding attention—it's about creating belief.
- Build assets that are difficult to steal—like your mindset, character, and personality.
- Titles can be taken. Positions can be reassigned. But who you are will always lead before what you hold.
- True leadership doesn't come from power.
- It comes from purpose—and the kind of person you choose to become.

Reflections:

- Are your people following your position or your principles?

- Do they comply because they must—or contribute because they want to?
- Are you chasing control or cultivating commitment?

"Leadership is not about commanding from the top—it's about inspiring from within. When people feel trusted and empowered, they don't just follow—they rise."

– Unknown

08

Master the Art of Selective Attention

*Learn to Ignore the Noise and Focus on
What Truly Matters*

In today's hyper-connected world, attention is currency—and distractions are everywhere. But leadership demands focus. The ability to sift through the noise and give energy only to what truly matters isn't just a skill—it's survival.

The Power of Focus

The Bhagavad Gita offers one of the most timeless lessons in mastering selective attention.

At the very start of the epic battle of Kurukshetra, Arjuna—one of the greatest warriors—stood frozen. He was overwhelmed. The enemy lines weren't just opponents; they were family, teachers, and friends. His vision blurred with emotion, and his grip on the bow loosened. He told Krishna, *"I will not fight."*

This wasn't weakness. It was mental chaos. Arjuna, though capable, was paralyzed by distraction—by guilt, attachment, and imagined consequences.

In response, Krishna didn't simplify the battlefield. He sharpened Arjuna's focus.

He said: *"Be steadfast in yoga, O Arjuna. Perform your duty and abandon all attachment to success or failure."*—Bhagavad Gita 2.48

Krishna reminded Arjuna of his *swadharma*—his personal duty—and taught him to let go of outcomes, emotional noise, and what others might think. That moment was a turning point. Arjuna shifted from hesitation to conviction, not because the war changed, but because his mind did.

The battlefield is a metaphor for life. Noise is inevitable—emails, meetings, opinions, pressure, judgment. But selective attention is the weapon that clears the fog.

As leaders, we can learn from Arjuna's moment. It's not about tuning out everything. It's about tuning in to what matters most. The project that moves the needle. The person who needs your time. The decision that aligns with your values.

Don't aim to do more. Aim to do what matters—and do it well.

My Story: When Comparison Becomes Noise

As I reflect on my journey, I realize that the true key to mastering selective attention lies in understanding this simple truth: "Don't trade your authenticity for approval." This insight, learned through both personal experience and guidance, became the cornerstone of my growth. Shortly after joining a new organization, I found myself in an uncomfortable situation. I had been hired to replace a well-regarded associate—but there was no transition, no overlap, and no real insight into how he operated. In my very first conversation, my manager said, *"Just so you know, you'll be compared with your predecessor—in both behaviour and delivery. It's part of our culture."*

I nodded. But inside, I was shaken.

Compared? To someone I've never met? Based on whose lens? How do I match up to a ghost?

For weeks, that thought consumed me. I kept wondering if I was doing things "right," which really meant—am I doing it the way he would've done it? I felt like I was living someone else's role, walking a path that wasn't mine.

In a moment of mental fatigue, I reached out to a leadership coach and she asked me a simple question:

"Why are you trying to become someone you don't even know?"

That hit me like a bolt. Why was I trying to mimic a stranger at the cost of my own personality, values, and instincts?

Around that time, I also recalled something my previous manager once told me:

"Every new person brings their own rhythm to the role. There's no golden standard—only results and relationships that work."

That was my turning point. I stopped obsessing over how my predecessor did things. I started tuning out the comparisons and tuned in to what I could bring to the table. I focused on doing the work in my own way—with authenticity, integrity, and clarity.

Yes, the early days were tough. The mental tug-of-war didn't vanish overnight. But slowly, the shift happened. My work started speaking for itself. My relationships found their footing. And eventually, people stopped bringing up the past—not because I erased it, but because I replaced it with something present and valuable.

That experience taught me this: comparison is noise. Trying to meet invisible expectations only muffles your strengths. The real challenge is not to fit a mold—but to stand tall in your own shape.

The Micromanagement Trap: A Senior Leader's Journey to Focus

At a prominent multinational corporation, a senior leader, known for his decisiveness, believed that his rapid responses to challenges were a sign of strong leadership. Whether it was a client issue, a product delay, or a team conflict, he was always quick to step in and make decisions. On the surface, this seemed like a strength—someone who acted fast and kept things moving. However, the leader's immediate engagement in every situation soon created unintended consequences.

As time passed, his approach began to backfire. The team's confidence started to erode. Every time the leader swooped in to provide answers, it undermined the work and strategies of the team. Well-thought-out plans were hijacked, and critical decisions were often made without considering the input of those who were closest to the problems. Instead of fostering collaboration, the leader's instinct to take control created confusion and stifled innovation. What had initially seemed like leadership was becoming micromanagement.

In a pivotal conversation with a trusted mentor, the leader reflected, "*I thought I was helping by solving problems quickly, but I see now that I'm causing more confusion. My intention was to guide, not control—but somewhere along the way, I lost sight of what really matters.*"

That moment of introspection was the turning point. The leader realized that his constant intervention was not allowing his team to focus on what mattered most. Instead of being everywhere and responding to everything, he needed to hone his attention on the areas where he could truly make an impact. It wasn't about solving every problem—it was about empowering the team to solve their own.

The leader then shifted his approach. He created a clearer framework for where his involvement was necessary and where his team should take the lead. He began practicing selective attention—ignoring the distractions of minor issues and focusing his energy on high-priority matters that would drive long-term success. He empowered his team by providing them with the autonomy to make decisions, offering guidance only when it truly added value.

The results were transformative. The team grew more confident, more collaborative, and more accountable. Instead of feeling stifled by constant oversight, they thrived with greater ownership and creative freedom. The leader, now focused on what truly mattered, shifted from being a micromanager to a strategic coach, guiding from behind and letting the team take the reins.

This version emphasizes the leader's realization of the importance of focusing on what truly matters and the value of selective attention in leadership, while also showcasing the shift from micromanagement to empowering the team.

Key Takeaways:

- Focus is not just about what you look at—it's about what you choose to ignore.
- Just as Arjuna in the Bhagavad Gita learned to see beyond relationships and emotions to focus on his dharma, we too must train ourselves to separate noise from necessity.
- Leadership clarity comes when we stop reacting to distractions—whether comparisons, opinions, or old benchmarks—and begin acting with intention.
- Selective attention is not about being blind—it's about being intentional.
- Leadership isn't about being everywhere—it's about being present where it matters most.

Reflections:

- What noise have you been tuning into lately that's clouding your focus?
- Are you being unconsciously driven by comparisons or invisible expectations?
- What might shift in your leadership if you allowed yourself to fully trust your own instincts and values?
- Am I spending my energy where it truly counts, or am I just trying to be seen as busy?

"The successful warrior is the average man, with laser-like focus."

– Bruce Lee

09

Balance is Not a Luxury, it's a Leadership Necessity

Work-life harmony starts at the top

Not long ago, someone asked me, *"How do you manage work-life balance?"*

I chuckled and replied, *"What's that? Aren't they the same?"*

The look on his face told me he thought I was joking. But I wasn't—not entirely.

For me, balance isn't about measuring work and life in equal parts. It's about integration—being fully present where I am, whether in a meeting or at my child's recital. It's about recognizing that balance isn't a destination, but a rhythm we learn to dance to.

The Story of My Missed Call

It was a warm Saturday evening—the kind you look forward to all week. My family had gathered to celebrate a milestone birthday. Laughter echoed from the living room. My daughter was about to perform something she'd been rehearsing for days.

And just then, my phone buzzed.

A client escalation. Urgent. Unexpected.

"*Just five minutes,*" I told all, stepping away to take the call.

By the time I returned, the performance was over. So was the moment.

I told myself it was unavoidable—and maybe it was. But what haunted me wasn't the decision itself. It was that I hadn't really made one. I had reacted, not led.

That evening never left me—not as guilt, but as a quiet turning point. It forced me to confront a question I hadn't dared to ask: *What kind of life am I leading—and modelling?*

That missed moment became my wake-up call. Since then, I've made a quiet but firm promise to myself: I will show up. Not just for work, but for my daughters—for our stories, our laughter, our rituals. Whether it's a school performance, a silly bedtime tale, or a heart-to-heart after a long day, an evening stroll with my wife, a call with my mother—I make space for it. Not because I have more time, but because I've learned to protect what truly matters by prioritizing with intention.

And at work, I flipped the script. I stopped trying to be everywhere, and started building a team that didn't need me to be. I focused on empowerment—giving people room to lead, make decisions, and grow. I made myself available, but not indispensable. Because real leadership isn't about how much you hold—It's about how much you release.

Today, I don't measure success by how busy I am. I measure it by how calmly I can step away—and know that everything will still move forward.

Balance Begins with What We Remove

Often, when we talk about balance, we focus on what more we can add—more family time, more breaks, more flexibility. But real balance often begins with subtraction.

Workplaces are filled with rituals and routines that may have outlived their purpose—status meetings without substance, rigid schedules for the sake of appearances, policies that value presence over performance. When we cling to these out of habit or hierarchy, we unknowingly create pressure points that erode well-being.

Leadership, then, is also about questioning what no longer serves us.

Do we need that daily check-in—or can it be replaced with a shared update that respects everyone's time? Is it necessary to enforce rigid hybrid work rules—or can we trust our people to deliver while honouring their personal rhythms?

Even our best intentions can backfire if we aren't careful. In our effort to keep associates engaged and help them grow, we often flood calendars with development activities, training sessions, and initiatives. While the intent is noble—upskilling and retention—too much of it, especially without breathing room, can become overwhelming. What begins as empowerment can start to feel like pressure if not paced with empathy.

I remember a week-long management development program organized for the talent pool including my team. It was well-structured and covered a wide range of leadership topics. But as the sessions progressed, I noticed that instead of being immersed in the discussions, many of the participants were quietly catching up on their routine emails or stepping out for calls. It wasn't that they lacked interest in self-development—in fact, these were some of the most committed individuals I know. But the content didn't align with their real-time challenges. And because their day-to-day work didn't pause, they were left juggling between the program and their core responsibilities.

By the end of the week, rather than returning with renewed energy or insights, they came back more exhausted than when they started. This wasn't learning—it was layering. We had unintentionally taken away time from their already stretched bandwidth, cutting into not just their work focus but also their personal space.

That experience was a wake-up call—for how organizations should approach development. Learning must not come at the cost of well-being. Programs designed to build people must also respect their time, energy, and mental load. Development is meaningful only when it supports—not sabotages—work-life balance.

Hybrid work, especially, offers us a powerful opportunity to reimagine how work fits into life—not the other way around.

Flexibility doesn't mean compromise. It means trusting people to manage their energy, not just their hours. It means acknowledging that productivity looks different for different people—and that comfort is not the enemy of commitment.

This shift is not just a trend—it's a necessity. The myth that work can only happen from an office has been decisively busted. The pandemic proved that with the right trust, tools, and clarity, people can deliver outcomes from wherever they are. Now, the challenge lies in letting go of outdated assumptions and building systems that support flexibility without guilt. When done right, hybrid work doesn't weaken culture—it strengthens it by respecting people's lives and honouring their autonomy.

Balance is not a policy—it's a mindset. And often, the best way to create it is not by doing more, but by doing less—with greater intention.

Work Shouldn't Feel Like a War Zone

In my experience, the real issue has rarely been the workload itself. What wears people down is the pressure behind it—often unspoken, sometimes unnecessary. It's not the number of tasks that exhausts teams; it's the emotional weight they carry while trying to deliver.

True leadership lies in creating an environment where even high expectations don't feel like a burden. Getting big things done without crushing spirits—that's not easy, but it's entirely possible.

A wise man once shared a metaphor that has stayed with me. He said: *"Managing a team is like maintaining an aquarium. You don't control the fish—you maintain the environment. If the water is clean and the ecosystem is healthy, the fish will thrive on their own."*

It was a brilliant analogy. Leadership isn't about micromanagement; it's about creating conditions in which people can breathe, grow, and perform without constant intervention. If the environment is toxic—clouded with stress, ambiguity, and unrealistic demands—no amount of talent will truly shine.

That's where work-life balance comes in. Balance isn't about working less—it's about creating a healthy atmosphere where performance is sustainable and people are treated like human beings, not just resources. Leaders who focus on nurturing this environment empower their teams to thrive, not just survive.

Balance Is Leadership

Leadership is a daily act of balancing:

- Between driving results and nurturing relationships
- Between pushing for excellence and pausing for well-being
- Between raising the bar and letting people catch their breath

It's not about micromanaging time. It's about creating the conditions where people can manage themselves—with clarity, confidence, and care.

If we want our teams to thrive—not just today, but consistently—we must stop treating balance as a bonus. It's a necessity. And like most cultural shifts, it starts with us.

Key Takeaways

- Work-life balance isn't a fixed formula; it's a flexible rhythm led by awareness and intention.
- True leadership involves creating environments where high performance and well-being can coexist.
- The best leaders manage pressure so it fuels, not fractures.
- Balance is not about perfection—it's about presence.
- Balance isn't about doing everything—it's about doing what truly matters.

Reflection:

- Are you reacting to your calendar, or choosing how you show up each day?
- Are you modelling balance for your team—or accidentally modelling burnout?
- Are there meetings or expectations in your work life that you continue simply out of habit?
- And more personally—what are you postponing in your life today that won't wait forever?

"You can't pour from an empty cup. Take care of yourself first—then lead others."

– Unknown

10

Lead with Empathy, Not Just Authority

Empathy Unlocks Initiative, Ownership, and Growth

Leadership is often perceived as the act of guiding others toward a goal—setting direction, correcting course, offering feedback, and driving performance. While all of this is true, leadership in its most transformative form is not just about offering critical insights and constructive feedback—It's about delivering them with the right tone and intent.

True leadership respects the self-worth and dignity of every individual. It's about ensuring that your guidance empowers rather than demotivates, lifts rather than flattens. And there is no better tool to do this than empathy.

The Story That Stole the Moment

As is the case every year, a student reached out to me for an internship opportunity. Since all my slots were already filled, I referred her to a colleague. I wasn't formally involved in her project, but I later learned that she was working on something I was quite familiar with.

A month passed, and I began to sense that she was struggling. It wasn't my responsibility—but it was my instinct as a leader to check in. So, I called her, casually, just to see how she was doing.

What started as a light conversation quickly turned into a deep, emotional one. She was frustrated and overwhelmed, trying to navigate a complex project with little to no guidance. She felt completely alone.

I paused. I listened. And then I asked her to walk me through what she had done so far. Within minutes, I could identify where she was stuck. I explained the fundamentals of the project and helped her understand the broader landscape—far beyond the immediate deliverables.

That's when I saw the shift. Her shoulders relaxed. Her eyes lit up. Confusion turned into clarity, and helplessness into confidence. We mapped out a way forward, and she left with renewed energy and direction.

What stayed with me the most wasn't the work we accomplished—it was her simple, heartfelt parting words: *"God bless you, Sir."*

That single sentence reminded me of the quiet power of empathy. It's not always about being in charge. Sometimes it's just about being there.

The Human Core of Leadership

In the workplace, true seniority isn't defined by titles. It's defined by the depth of experience, knowledge, and maturity that individuals bring—and by the kindness and courage they show in using that power to uplift others.

Leadership is a unique art of dealing effectively with people's feelings. Trying to manage it scientifically—with only data—may be a limiting approach. Empathy builds trust, enhances collaboration, and elevates morale by genuinely considering the needs and emotions of others.

And yet, many workplaces confuse professionalism with emotional detachment. But let's remember: professionalism does not mean we abandon humanity. Expressing anger when someone makes a mistake only teaches them to hide it next time. Demeaning someone does not bring out their best—it drives fear, not growth. Sometimes, just a constructive discussion with a collaborative intention works wonders. Try—and see the result.

I've seen this truth unfold in my own experience. There was a time in my career when I had a significant difference in opinion with my manager. That wasn't unusual—disagreements happen. What mattered more was how it was handled.

Instead of engaging in a meaningful dialogue to understand the reasoning behind our divergent approaches, the conversation became one-sided. The objective, clearly, was not to align or improve—it was to shake my confidence and demean me. Even though my approach had begun showing positive outcomes, it did not align with my manager's expectations. The result? A conversation aimed not at growth, but at proving me wrong.

I stood by my intent and integrity, but I could see how such interactions—repeated over time—can push even strong, capable people to the edge. When confidence is eroded systematically, when dignity is not protected, people don't just lose motivation—they leave. Not because they want to, but because the emotional cost becomes too high. And often, they leave with unfinished stories and unspoken sadness.

This is the silent damage that poor leadership can cause. And this is why empathy isn't a nice-to-have—it's non-negotiable. Leadership is not a test of dominance—it's a test of emotional intelligence. The goal is not to win arguments or enforce conformity, but to build trust, respect, and alignment. When people feel heard, supported, and safe, they don't just stay—they thrive.

The Empathy Cycle: The Soul of Effective Leadership

Empathy in leadership is not a one-way gesture—it is the catalyst for a powerful cycle. When leaders lead with genuine care, trust, and support, they unlock a response that no authority can command: deep commitment, personal ownership, and sustained passion. This empathy cycle fosters a self-motivated, resilient, and collaborative work environment where creativity, accountability, and human connection thrive. But empathy doesn't just power performance—it defines our humanity.

In addition to "empathy by leadership", "empathy for leadership" is equally vital. It's easy to expect compassion and understanding from those in charge, but leadership, too, comes with its own share of pressure. The responsibility to steer teams, make tough decisions, drive results, and maintain organizational growth often rests on their shoulders. Leaders are human—they navigate uncertainty, carry emotional weight, and balance expectations from all sides. When team members recognize this, offer support, and extend patience, they contribute to a culture of mutual respect and shared ownership. That's when the empathy cycle truly closes—not just flowing top-down but circulating across the organization. The people who see this bigger picture are already on the path to becoming great leaders themselves. Because in the end, empathy isn't just a leadership trait—it's the soul of effective leadership and the foundation of a thriving workplace.

Key Takeaways:

- Empathy empowers. When people feel understood and supported, they become more confident, creative, and accountable.
- Leadership is human-centric. It is about showing up, not just standing above. It's about helping even when it's not your job to help.
- Constructive conversations matter. Demeaning others may create compliance, but empathy fosters genuine growth and loyalty.
- Trust and empowerment spark the empathy cycle. What you give as a leader often returns to you multiplied in the form of commitment and initiative.

- Titles don't define leadership. Experience, maturity, humility, and a service mindset do.
- Humanity belongs in professionalism. Being kind, curious, and emotionally available doesn't weaken leadership—it strengthens it.

Reflections:

- Think of a time when someone showed you empathy at work. How did it impact your confidence or performance?
- When was the last time you listened to a teammate beyond just their task update? What did you learn about their perspective or challenges?
- Do your team members feel safe to express their struggles and ideas to you? How can you create more psychological safety?
- Have you ever dismissed a concern because it wasn't "your responsibility"? What might have changed if you had leaned in with empathy instead?
- Are your corrections and feedback empowering or demoralizing? How can you adjust your tone and approach to better support growth?
- What systems or habits can you build into your leadership style to consistently practice empathy, not just in crises but every day?

"Empathy doesn't make leadership soft—it makes it strong, trusted, and unforgettable."

– From the Author

11

Let Go of the Old That No Longer Serves

Challenge traditions and practices that hinder progress.

In many organizations, departments function like isolated islands—each focused solely on its own objectives, timelines, and responsibilities. While this structure can bring clarity, it often comes at a cost: limited communication, disconnected ideas, and a lack of empathy. Even the most capable teams can find themselves working at cross purposes, solving symptoms instead of addressing root causes, and missing opportunities for collaboration.

Breaking Down Silos: A Shift from "My Work" to "Our Success"

When I first took on the responsibility as a project manager, I was excited by the immense talent we had across the organization—sharp minds in R&D, detail-oriented regulatory experts, resourceful procurement leads, efficient manufacturing professionals and customer-savvy sales professionals. And yet, despite this deep bench strength, something was off. Every team was busy, but not always in sync. The R&D team would finish formulation trials only to find the regulatory pathway hadn't been explored. Sales would pitch features that didn't exist in the current product design. Procurement struggled with last-minute raw material specifications because they hadn't been looped in early enough. It wasn't incompetence— it was isolation. Each department operated like a silo, efficient within its walls but disconnected from the bigger picture.

The unwritten rule was clear: "*Stick to your lane.*" But as market demands rapidly evolved, I realized we could no longer afford to move sequentially—we had to move collaboratively. So, I started challenging this mindset—not just within my team, but across the entire organization.

This shift wasn't easy. I began with small but intentional steps. During a project meeting, I invited the sales team to a technical formulation meeting. Initially, eyebrows were raised. "Why are they here?" someone whispered. But within minutes, a sales manager shared a customer pain point that completely shifted our direction. The R&D team improvised the process—something we hadn't even considered.

In another instance, our regulatory colleague flagged a documentation requirement just a week before launch. By involving her earlier in the process next time, we avoided last-minute scrambles. Procurement was looped in ahead of time, which helped them secure better vendor deals and reduce lead times. Slowly but surely, the gears began to turn in unison.

It wasn't always smooth sailing. Some team members were hesitant to change, feeling more comfortable in their well-established roles. But I reminded them: the best services aren't built by specialists working in isolation—they're built by teams who understand each other's constraints, contributions, and language. One of our biggest successes came when we delivered our project as per customer's expectations. This wasn't just a delivery—it was a transformation. By involving every function from the start, we delivered a lineup that was more customer-centric, cost-effective, and easier to scale. The customer's response was exceptional, and internally, our culture began to shift. Teams that had previously worked in silos were now volunteering to collaborate.

The old, siloed way of working had served its time, but as we let go of the outdated structure, we saw results that were far beyond what any individual department could have achieved on its own. The shift from "my work" to "our success" changed everything. It was no longer about protecting our individual turf—it was about building something greater, together.

And that's when I truly understood; collaboration isn't a task—it's a habit. Once you break down the silos, the solutions become smarter, faster, and more impactful. Innovation doesn't happen in departments; it happens in conversations. And as leaders, it's our job to create those conversations.

A Glimpse into a Candid Interview

In this brief yet revealing exchange, we meet a leader who embodies clarity, optimism, and self-awareness. As the conversation unfolds, we gain insight into a leadership philosophy that values strength over self-criticism, purpose over perfection, and evolution over old mindsets. This is not just an interview—it's a window into the mindset of someone who chooses to lead by lifting others and letting go of what no longer serves.

Interviewer: *If I were to ask your colleagues or team members about your key strengths, what do you think they'd say?*

Candidate: *I believe they'd describe me as an enabler and a coach—someone who fosters collaboration and empowers people to perform at their best. I'm often seen as a structured thinker and an optimist who brings energy, clarity, and momentum to any project. They'd probably also say I'm approachable and trustworthy—someone who's always available to listen, reflect, and contribute meaningfully.*

Interviewer: *That's impressive. And are there any areas you think you need to work on?*

Candidate: (smiles after a thoughtful pause) *I've let go of the old belief that we must constantly "fix" our weaknesses to succeed. I focus on deepening my strengths, because that's where I create the most value. Of course, I stay aware of areas for improvement, especially if something is holding me back. But I don't dwell on what's missing unless it truly impacts my effectiveness. A bird doesn't waste time trying to run—it soars because it understands the power of its wings.*

Interviewer: *That's a refreshing perspective.*

Candidate: *Thank you. I believe success comes from knowing what to let go of—and old mindsets that no longer serve are often the first things we need to leave behind.*

Key Takeaways:

- Don't fight outdated systems—learn how to navigate and transform them.
- Old mindsets can be the biggest obstacles to progress. Letting go of them creates space for innovation.
- Collaboration across boundaries leads to richer, more relevant solutions.
- Soft skills are not optional—they are essential.
- Play to your strengths. Improve weaknesses only if they hinder growth.

Reflection:

- Think about one outdated belief or practice you're holding onto—whether in your personal, academic, or professional life.
- What would it look like to let it go? What new possibilities might open up?

"The measure of intelligence is the ability to change."

—Albert Einstein

12

Create Leaders, Not Dependents

Empower others to think, act, and lead independently.

In candid conversations with senior leaders, I often hear a familiar sentiment: *"At this stage of my career, my job is to make the team work and achieve deliverables."*

The intent is admirable—but the approach warrants reflection. There's a subtle yet powerful difference between a managerial mindset and a leadership perspective. What if, instead of focusing on *"making the team work,"* we embraced the mindset of *"letting the team work"*?

This isn't about stepping back—it's about stepping aside with intent. It's about creating space with just the right amount of guidance so that ownership, trust, and growth can flourish. It's a quiet yet powerful signal of belief in your team—in their capability, judgment, and intrinsic drive.

When leaders adopt this stance, something magical happens: people bring far more to the table than any one leader could orchestrate alone. Their creativity and commitment are unlocked. Their independence matures. And perhaps most importantly, leaders are freed to focus on strategic dimensions rather than micromanaging every detail.

Sometimes, the most impactful leadership lies not in stepping up—but in knowing when to step aside.

The Lion and the Law of Wasted Efforts

In the vast savannah, a lioness crouches low, eyes fixed on a herd of antelope. Muscles tensed, she waits for the perfect moment. She charges—swift and powerful—but the antelopes scatter. The hunt ends in dust and empty jaws. She pants, watches the herd disappear, then retreats. Tomorrow, she will try again.

What many don't realize is that lioness fail in about 75% of their hunts. That means, out of every four attempts, only one ends in a meal. Yet she doesn't sulk, blame the wind, or give up. She keeps going—because her instinct understands something most humans forget: wasted effort is not wasted growth.

This is what biologist and author Laurence Gonzales refers to as the "Law of Wasted Effort"—the principle that success in nature is built on countless unsuccessful attempts. It's not inefficiency; it's resilience in motion. Fish lay thousands of eggs, but only a few hatch. Trees release countless seeds, most of which will never take root. Baby bears face a perilous path—many never reach adulthood. Yet nature keeps trying. It accepts loss as part of creation.

As leaders, we often do the opposite. We try to protect our teams from failure. We over-direct, over-approve, and over-control.

In seeking efficiency and certainty, we create environments where people become hesitant to try—afraid to fail.

In my early leadership journey, I worked with a brilliant but hesitant team member. She had ideas, energy, and insight—but always waited for validation. Every pitch began with, "Do you think this will work?" It wasn't ability she lacked—it was confidence. She was conditioned to seek permission, not to take ownership.

One day, I handed her a project I couldn't fully define and said, "Take the lead. Fail if you must, but I trust you to find your way." She looked terrified. But she did it. Not perfectly—but with accountability, with mistakes, and with learning. Today, she's someone others turn to for guidance.

That's the essence: leaders are not built in safety—they're forged in action through effort, uncertainty and failure.

Creating leaders means making room for wasted efforts—because those "failures" become the foundation of independence, resilience, and true leadership.

So, the next time someone on your team stumbles, resist the urge to rescue. Let them hunt again. Let them build instinct. Don't just give direction—give them the space to lead.

A True Professional Pays It Forward

A true professional isn't defined merely by their ability to overcome challenges or chase ambitious goals. The hallmark of real professionalism lies in the ability to lift others while climbing—sharing strength, offering guidance, and multiplying impact through generosity. That's how we create a ripple effect of growth, where every success story sparks another.

After years of industrial experience, I felt a strong pull to reconnect with academia—the space where my journey began. Students today crave more than theory; they want context, perspective, and a bridge between textbooks and real-world challenges. They seek relevance. They seek an answer for the "*why*" and the "*how*," not just the "*what.*".

Today's students are tomorrow's problem solvers, and what they crave most is relevance—how the concepts they learn translate to industrial application, how to think critically in ambiguity, and how to adapt with confidence. By sharing case studies, project experiences, and hard-earned lessons from the trenches of industry, I aim to bring that relevance to the classroom. There's a quiet joy in watching young minds light up when they see how knowledge connects with reality. That's where true impact begins—not just in what we build, but in who we empower.

I often collaborate with professors and researchers—offering mentoring, sharing industrial perspectives, and even providing samples of specialized chemicals they might require for experimentation. These small but meaningful acts help fuel innovation and build a much-needed bridge between research and practical application.

But beyond the immediate value, I see something deeper in these interactions: an opportunity to shape the leaders of tomorrow. By investing time, knowledge, and support today, I hope to empower these brilliant minds to grow not only as researchers but also as confident, grounded decision-makers when they eventually sit on the other side of the table. It's my quiet contribution to building a future where science and leadership go hand in hand.

And perhaps the most fulfilling moments are when I unexpectedly meet young professionals who say, *"Sir, you helped me when I needed it most—during my studies, when I was unsure, or when I was searching for direction."* That heartfelt gratitude, those quiet acknowledgments, fill me with a deep sense of purpose. It reminds me that real success isn't just measured by what we achieve—but by the lives we touch along the way.

When you help others grow, you don't just build a legacy—you build a future.

Turning Pressure into Performance

In high-performance cultures, stress is inevitable—but it doesn't have to be harmful. When channelled through purpose and thoughtful execution, stress becomes a catalyst for growth, not a trigger for fear. The key lies in how leaders shape the experience. Instead of pressure to prove oneself or please others, we must foster a culture where the challenge is exciting, and the goal is shared success. That transformation begins with mindset. We need to move from managing tasks to mentoring thought processes—guiding teams to harness stress as fuel for innovation and self-improvement. This shift is most effective when paired with intelligent work practices: meticulous planning, deep thinking, strategic collaboration, timely follow-ups, smart time management, and the embrace of technology. A positive, enabling environment completes the picture—where individuals don't just deliver output, but lead with clarity, vision, and care. That's how we turn pressure into performance—and build resilient, high-impact teams in the process.

Key Takeaways:

- Empowered teams thrive when leaders step aside with trust—not control.
- Wasted efforts are a necessary part of growth. Let your people learn through doing.
- True leadership is not about protecting others from failure—it's about guiding them through it.
- Professionalism isn't complete without giving back. Mentoring and supporting academia enrich both industry and education.
- Stress isn't the enemy. Fear is. Purpose-driven pressure unlocks potential.

Reflections:

- Where might you be over-directing your team? How can you create more space for them to lead?
- Have you been too focused on deliverables instead of development?
- Who can you mentor today from your journey so far?

- How can you contribute to the academic world or early-stage professionals this month?
- Are you helping your team channel stress as purpose— or letting it morph into pressure?

"Leadership is not about being indispensable. It's about making others capable."

– From the author

13

Transparency Builds Trust, Silence Breaks It

Why Open Communication Is Your Greatest Credibility Tool

One critical aspect of leadership is communication—specifically, the ability to communicate openly, transparently, and consistently. I've had the privilege of working with managers who understood the power of dialogue—those who asked questions, listened deeply, and created space for others to express themselves. With them, trust felt natural. You could bring your whole self to work because you knew you were heard.

But I've also had the opposite experience—and it's one I won't forget.

The Silence That Spoke the Loudest

There was a time in my career when I reported to a manager with whom I struggled to establish even the most basic level of communication. Our conversations were strictly professional, often reduced to rapid-fire exchanges of instructions and deadlines. There was no space for reflection, feedback, or even a moment of informal human connection. Everything was about him—his updates, his advice, his stories, his perspective. I was expected to listen, accept, execute, and move on.

The tone was always brisk, and the rhythm unrelenting. If I missed a call, even for a legitimate reason, reconnecting was difficult. The window of opportunity would shut abruptly, and I would be left catching up—often guessing at the expectations. There was no room for, *"How are you doing?"* or *"What are you struggling with?"* or even *"Do you have any thoughts on this?"*

This lack of communication didn't just affect my motivation—it chipped away my confidence. I began second-guessing myself, holding back ideas, and shrinking into compliance. I didn't feel seen. I didn't feel safe. And I certainly didn't feel trusted.

I remember one particularly incident that stayed with me—not because I missed an opportunity, but because of the insensitivity that surrounded it.

We were gearing up for an important internal event that involved all key stakeholders, including the business head. I had prepared a crisp, well-thought-out presentation. It was my first chance to present directly in front of the business head, and I was genuinely excited. I had spent days putting the slides together—researching, designing, rehearsing—ensuring that I could deliver with clarity and conviction. My manager, who was responsible for driving the event, was fully aware of how much this presentation meant to me.

What I didn't know, however, was that the business head had another commitment and would have to leave right after lunch. My manager knew this yet said nothing. Worse, despite having ample time in the pre-lunch session, he made no effort to ensure my short presentation was slotted in. It wasn't about being sidelined or missing the spotlight—what stung was the casual disregard, the absence of even the smallest gesture of consideration.

That moment revealed something deeper: when your aspirations are treated as dispensable, when your presence is acknowledged but your priorities are ignored, it creates a quiet erosion of trust. It wasn't a matter of hierarchy—it was a matter of humanity. And in environments where sensitivity is missing, even the most capable voices can begin to fall silent.

Speak to Express, Not Impress

While sharing ideas, people often lean heavily on jargon to impress. But in doing so, they often forget to express. Somewhere between sounding intelligent and being understood, the essence of their message gets lost. The truth is—clarity always trumps complexity. Simplicity isn't a lack of intellect; it's a sign of maturity, empathy, and respect for the audience.

I recall a particularly vivid example involving two customers— both senior leaders at competing pharmaceutical companies, both working on nearly identical projects. Let's call them Mr. Fluent and Mr. Clear.

Mr. Fluent, a well-read, impeccably polished executive, spoke English with such flair that he could've been mistaken for a TED speaker. Unfortunately, that gift of language was also his curse. Our meetings felt like decoding a linguistic puzzle. Sentences were peppered with "synergistic alignment," "scalable ideation," "multivariate optimization"—all strung together so elaborately that I often lost track of the actual topic.

At times, I found myself nodding politely while mentally whispering, *"Wait, what are we even solving here?"* Once, after a particularly long monologue involving three frameworks and two paradigms, I had to sheepishly ask, "Could you just tell me what you need the excipient to actually do?"

Contrast this with Mr. Clear. His approach was refreshingly different: simple, direct, and outcome focused. "Here's the dosage form, here's the issue we're facing, and here's where we need your help," he said in our very first meeting. No fireworks, no linguistic somersaults—just good old clarity.

The result? I could get back to Mr. Clear with a solution within days, while Mr. Fluent's project stretched over months of circular conversations. The irony? They were both racing to launch the same formulation. Guess who crossed the finish line first.

It's a story I often smile about, not just because it taught me the value of clear communication—but because it was also a reminder that intelligence doesn't always need a thesaurus.

Trust and Transparency: The Real Drivers of Motivation and Collaboration

One of the simplest, most powerful ways to keep your team engaged is by trusting their intentions. Scepticism breeds silence—people shut down when they feel second-guessed or constantly questioned. I witnessed this firsthand with a young colleague who initially hesitated to share her ideas, fearing she would be picked apart. But when I made it a point to demonstrate consistent trust in her judgment, she began to open—slowly at first, and then with growing confidence. Over time, she stepped into a key project and delivered beyond expectations. Trust doesn't just build morale—it activates potential and inspires people to grow.

But trust alone isn't enough. It thrives in an environment of transparency—one where people feel safe to be open, honest, and human. One of my managers said to me, *"Are you having sleepless nights? Then try being honest and transparent throughout the day—see how peacefully you sleep. It's just a matter of practice."* That advice stayed with me because it underscored a powerful truth: transparency isn't just about how others perceive you; it's about the peace you create within yourself. And that peace becomes contagious in a team. When people feel seen, trusted, and included in open conversations, collaboration becomes natural.

Moreover, I've learned that transparency also grows in the company of great minds. If you want to be respected as a genius, surround yourself with geniuses. True leadership isn't about having all the answers—it's about having the humility to recognize and elevate the brilliance in others. When trust and transparency go hand in hand, you create not just high-performing teams, but high-trust cultures that attract and retain top talent.

Key Takeaways:

- Silence erodes trust – When communication is one-way or absent, it diminishes morale, motivation, and psychological safety.
- Trust inspires initiative – When people feel trusted, they take ownership, share ideas, and rise to the occasion.
- Transparency breeds peace – Being honest and open reduces inner conflict and builds authentic relationships.
- Clarity outperforms cleverness – Simple, direct communication drives results more effectively than jargon-filled monologues.
- Genius multiplies in good company – True leaders surround themselves with other brilliant minds and lift them up.

Reflections:

- Have I unintentionally created a communication gap with someone on my team? What can I do today to reopen that channel?
- When was the last time I trusted someone before they "earned" it? What happened?

- Do I speak to impress or to express? How might I simplify my message without diluting its strength?
- What daily habits can help me become more transparent in my leadership style?
- Who around me is doing great work quietly? How can I give them more voice and visibility?

"If you can't explain it simply, you don't understand it well enough."

– Albert Einstein

14

Celebrate Progress, Not Just Perfection

Encouraging Growth Over Flawlessness

As I step into another professional year, I'm filled with deep gratitude for my team. What drove our success wasn't flawless strategies or picture-perfect execution—it was the steady rhythm of everyday contributions, offered without waiting for conditions to be ideal.

We built our journey brick by brick—through small steps, quiet persistence, and subtle shifts in mindset. Each action may have seemed minor in isolation, but together, they created something truly meaningful. It's like assembling a sandwich: one slice of bread won't fill you up, but add a bit of cheese, some lettuce, maybe a slice of tomato—and suddenly, you have a meal that satisfies.

It reminds me of the timeless song from *Khatta Meetha*:

"Thoda hai, thode ki zarurat hai."

A line that beautifully echoes our spirit—not a hunger for what's missing, but an appreciation for what's already unfolding. Our progress wasn't always smooth, but we still chose to celebrate progress at every stage, instead of postponing our pride for some distant point of perfection.

Growth isn't always tidy. But it's real. And when we embrace it—even in its imperfect form—we build a culture where people feel safe to try, contribute, and evolve.

The Quiet Power of Trying

When I look back on my journey, I realize that my greatest victories didn't come dressed in perfection. They were born from showing up, trying again, adjusting course, and trusting the process. The world may applaud flawless execution, but I've learned that real leadership is built on the courage to take imperfect action—and keep going.

One such moment came when I pitched the idea of creating a product training module. It felt like something our organization desperately needed—like socks in a shoe sale. We didn't have all the data. We didn't have a fancy framework. But what we did have was enthusiasm, caffeine, and a team ready to roll.

So, we dove in. Built the first version with heart, hustle, and probably too many slides. We were proud—optimistic that our baby would mesmerize the crowd.

Well… the reaction was less standing ovation and more polite head tilt. Some folks found it too technical, others said it felt just OK. Did it sting? Of course. But instead of sulking in a corner, we took the feedback on the chin.

We scribbled notes, huddled again, reworked the flow, added practical examples, and trimmed the jargon. The second version had more zing. The third had actual engagement. Fast forward a few iterations—and boom! That humble prototype evolved into a robust, mandatory, and high-impact training program.

And it all started because we didn't wait for perfection—we just started. Slightly clueless, mostly excited, and totally committed.

That's what celebrating progress looks like. It's not just about success—it's about having the grit to learn in the open. Today, I encourage my team to do the same. When someone says, *"It's not perfect yet,"* I gently ask, *"But is it good enough to start?"* Because we don't grow by holding back—we grow by stepping forward, even when the ground is a little shaky.

So, here's to the rough first draft.

- To the expectation that didn't land.
- To the data that was inadequate for explanation.
- To the courage to try, revise, and try again.

Let's celebrate all of it. Because perfection may impress, but progress transforms.

Resilience in the Face of Recognition Gaps

There were several moments when we, as a team, truly deserved appreciation for the exceptional work we had done. And like any human being, we felt disappointed—even hurt—when that recognition didn't come. At first, it stung. We hadn't yet calibrated our expectations to the realities of our surroundings. But that feeling didn't last long. We gathered ourselves, laughed at the situation—and sometimes at our own emotional overreactions—and then did what we always do best: we bounced back.

Rather than dwell on the oversight, we chose to turn inward and uplift each other. We acknowledged every small contribution, celebrated one another's efforts, and made it a point to recognize not just our own teammates but colleagues across the organization. We pulled people into the spotlight whenever we could, reminding them—and ourselves—that recognition need not always come from the top.

We stopped checking how we were being perceived—because we knew we were on the right path.

And that little bit of belief, that shared understanding, was enough to keep the energy alive. We knew there was still so much more to achieve, and we weren't going to let the absence of applause dim our purpose.

I'm especially grateful for our scheduled team meetings—those regular sessions where we never missed a chance to openly and wholeheartedly appreciate one another for what truly mattered. I vividly recall how someone's quiet but relentless drive on a critical project was met with warm applause, or how another team member's behind-the-scenes support was finally brought into the spotlight. And I must admit, I was genuinely overwhelmed when my team turned their appreciation toward me—recognizing not just outcomes, but the intent and effort behind my leadership. These moments of genuine appreciation don't just celebrate milestones—they built trust, lift spirits, and remind us that recognizing progress, however small, fuels a culture of growth. Bottom of Form

Key Takeaways:

- Progress is built on consistent effort, not perfection.
- Acting before you feel "ready" opens the door to growth.
- Recognition is powerful, but self-worth and team appreciation matter just as much.
- Embracing imperfection creates a safe space for learning and innovation.
- Culture thrives when people celebrate progress—together and often.

Reflection Prompts:

- When was the last time you held back because something wasn't perfect?
- What small progress in your life or work deserves more recognition than it has received?
- How can you model "progress over perfection" for your team or peers this week?
- Are there areas where you or your team are waiting for external validation instead of celebrating internal growth?

"Progress, not perfection, is what turns effort into evolution"

– From the Author

15

Lead Tough Conversations with Grace

When opinions clash, true leadership aligns.

Some of the hardest conversations I've had in my career never began with shouting or confrontation. They began with silence. The kind that comes from mismatched expectations, brewing resentment, or a difference in values that no one dares to name. But I've learned—those silences speak the loudest. And leadership isn't about avoiding them. It is about entering the storm and steering through it with clarity, calm, and courage with intent to bring the best out of others.

The Role of Ego and the Power of Presence

One of the most crucial elements in navigating tough conversations—especially with your own team—is managing your ego. When someone challenges your actions or expresses disappointment, it's tempting to take it personally or react defensively. But leadership isn't about protecting your pride; it's about protecting the relationship.

If you can shift your perspective and receive the words as though they are meant for you, not against you, the conversation transforms. These moments are often when your teammates show their truest selves. Their guard drops, their truth spills out. And if the intent behind their words is genuine and non-malicious, what initially feels like confrontation becomes the foundation of trust.

A Moment I Almost Missed

I remember an incident that reinforced this truth deeply.

One day, I noticed a subtle but strange change in one of my teammates. She had always been energetic, involved, and full of warmth. But that day, she seemed distant. She wasn't engaging in team banter. She avoided eye contact. She kept her head down even during our informal catchups.

At first, I dismissed it. *"We all have our off days,"* I told myself. But something didn't sit right.

Later in the day, as I passed by her desk, I caught a glimpse of her eyes—red and moist. That's when I knew: this wasn't just a bad day.

I invited her gently for a chat and said, *"Is there something you want to share with me? Everything doesn't seem okay at your end."*

She sat down. Took a sip of water. Then slowly began to speak. *"I feel like you're keeping things from me,"* she said. *"I feel neglected."*

It could have hit me like an accusation. I could have responded coldly or dismissed her concerns. But what I heard behind her words wasn't blame—it was belonging. It was ownership.

She wanted to be included. She cared. And that, to me, was powerful.

I apologized sincerely. Not because I had done something wrong, but because her experience of feeling excluded deserved acknowledgment. Then I explained why certain decisions or conversations may have unintentionally made her feel left out.

And finally, I reassured her: *"Please don't hold back these thoughts in the future. Come to me. Let's talk it out."*

That conversation didn't just clear the air—it became the seed for a new, open culture. We initiated regular review meetings, more transparent sharing, and a culture of open dialogue. It made our team stronger, more cohesive, and more accountable.

Not all tough conversations are bad. If handled with humility and empathy, they can be the catalyst for transformation.

A Leader in the Making

Another experience that stays with me is with a teammate who consistently delivered outstanding results. He was well-behaved, diligent, and an undeniable asset to the organization. Over the years, he had earned immense trust and credibility.

But something changed when he was given a team to manage.

Soon, I began receiving complaints about his behavior. Words like "arrogance" and "insensitivity" surfaced. This was uncharacteristic—and unacceptable for the values we upheld in our department.

I decided to speak with him. After completing a routine project review, I gently asked if he was facing any challenges in his new role.

He immediately grew nervous. Defensive. *"Everything's fine,"* he said. *"All good."*

Sensing the wall going up, I calmly pointed to a few recent project outcomes that hadn't met expectations. Without naming anyone, I also shared that there had been concerns raised about his team interactions.

But he stood firm. *"All is well. The only issue is lack of support from cross functional teams,"* he replied.

I didn't stop there. I nudged him further.

That's when the truth began to unravel. Slowly, he admitted that the expectations from him had become overwhelming. Managing multiple-fronts people, projects, timelines—was proving far more challenging than he had anticipated.

I had already sensed this.

So, I told him something I wish someone had told me earlier in my career: *"You have already proven yourself as an individual contributor. But now, it's not just about what you can do. It's about what your team can do through you."*

I reminded him that there are only 24 hours in a day. More responsibility cannot mean longer hours forever. It must mean more working hands, more delegation, and more trust. His next growth leap would come not from personal excellence, but from building and enabling excellence in others.

That's when it clicked.

He realized that clinging to self-performance was holding him back. That true leadership was about building power beyond oneself.

Today, he's leading a larger team, driving projects with maturity and collaborative strength.

And the most interesting part?

That story is not just his. It's my story. Because I saw in him what I had once faced with myself. And sometimes, it takes a mirror to remind us of how far we've come—and how far we can help others go.

Key Takeaways:

- Tough conversations are not interruptions—they are leadership in motion.
- Managing your ego opens the door to real connection and resolution.
- Behind most complaints lies a desire to contribute meaningfully—if we listen.
- Growth often requires holding a mirror to ourselves and helping others do the same.
- Leadership is not about doing more; it's about enabling more through others.

Reflections:

- Is there a conversation you've been avoiding that could transform a relationship?
- Are you leading from a place of ego, or from a space of empathy and curiosity?
- When was the last time you paused to ask someone how they truly feel at work?
- Can you create the psychological safety needed for your team to speak up?

"In the crucible of tough conversations, leadership is forged. When we meet discomfort with curiosity, and defensiveness with humility, we create space for growth—ours and theirs. Sometimes, the most difficult talks become the most defining chapters in our journey."

– From the author

16

Gratitude Grounds Great Leadership

Stay Connected to Your People and Your Purpose

Who Is Your Krishna?

In the great Indian epic *Mahabharata*, Arjuna stood tall on his chariot in the heart of the Kurukshetra battlefield—calm, focused, and confident in his skills. As Karna unleashed wave after wave of arrows, Arjuna held his ground. Every successful defence seemed to reinforce the belief that it was his own talent carrying him through the storm.

But what Arjuna didn't notice—at least not yet—was the quiet presence that made all the difference.

Krishna, his charioteer, wasn't just guiding the horses. He was watching the battlefield closely, anticipating every twist and turn, shielding Arjuna from dangers that were invisible to him. He bore the weight of strategy and timing, without ever stepping into the spotlight.

To help Arjuna understand this, Krishna once stepped away from the chariot. In that moment, Karna's arrow hit with such force that the chariot shook violently. Arjuna was taken aback. It was a powerful reminder: it wasn't just his skill keeping him safe—it was Krishna's unseen effort, wisdom, and support.

That moment changed Arjuna's perspective. It was no longer just about personal prowess—it was about partnership, humility, and gratitude.

As leaders, we often celebrate outcomes and overlook those who quietly help us get there. So pause and reflect: Who is your Krishna?

Who helps you stay steady under pressure, navigate uncertainty, and continue forward—even when they get little recognition?

Leadership is not just about moving ahead—it's about remembering who helped you along the way. And expressing that gratitude, sincerely and often, keeps us grounded in both our purpose and our people.

Take Care of Those Who Walk with You

Take care of the people who make you feel happy and valued; they are rare treasures on this earth. I've realized that my ability to challenge limitations, think beyond the horizon, and execute efficiently doesn't come from some personal superpower—it comes from the people around me. My team and few good people. Their quiet strength, daily support, wisdom and shared commitment form the invisible scaffolding that holds everything up.

Leadership isn't about knowing all the answers. It's about walking the path with people who help you ask better questions. And for that, I'm endlessly grateful.

Great leadership is grounded in gratitude—both for the people who support us and for the opportunity to serve others. Like Krishna's presence on Arjuna's chariot, a leader's true strength lies not in personal power alone, but in the connection with and support from others. By nurturing your team, being present for them, and listening to their needs, you create an environment where growth is inevitable, and success is shared.

Servant Leadership: Empowering Through Service and Example

Great leadership isn't about commanding from the top—it's about serving with intention, humility, and gratitude. Servant leadership is rooted in the belief that true leaders elevate others, not by wielding power, but by sharing it. It's not about the team serving the leader—it's about the leader serving the team.

This leadership mindset resonates deeply with the spirit of gratitude, collaboration and connection. It recognizes that influence is earned through shared purpose, mutual respect, and authentic care. Servant leaders don't just guide from above—they roll up their sleeves and walk beside their people. They listen more than they speak, support more than they instruct, and empower more than they direct.

I remember a moment that brought this philosophy to life for me. We were at a critical juncture in our innovation pipeline. The product development team was tackling a tough formulation—one that demanded not just technical skill, but deep insight into excipients and process behaviour. Despite their commitment, progress was slow, and frustration was building.

During a check-in, I noticed the team huddled around a whiteboard, grappling with inconsistencies in the product development plan. The fatigue was visible. Though it wasn't expected of me to dive into the technical weeds, I couldn't stand by. I had faced similar challenges in the past, and I knew I had something to offer.

So, I pulled up a chair, asked a few pointed questions, and shared a relevant experience—how we had resolved a similar issue by using the right excipient and processing parameters. We dissected the process step by step, debated ideas, and ended the day with a promising experimental plan.

But I didn't stop there.

Over the next several days, I rolled up my sleeves—quite literally—and stepped back into the lab, a place I hadn't worked hands-on in for nearly 15 years since my days as a scientist. It was thrilling and humbling at the same time—like returning to an old battlefield where the tools had changed, but the spirit remained the same. I worked alongside our scientists, dirtying my hands in the formulation process. From batch preparations to reviewing outputs and troubleshooting in real time, I immersed myself fully. It wasn't just about solving the technical challenge—it was about modelling what shared responsibility looks like. It was about showing that no role is too small when the stakes are high and that real leadership sometimes means trading the conference room for the cleanroom. It was also about helping the team become intimately familiar with the process, boosting both their confidence and capability.

Later, one of the team members said, "It wasn't just the idea that helped—it was your willingness to stand beside us what mattered."

That moment reinforced my belief in servant leadership. True leadership is not staying on the pedestal—it's descending the ladder when needed, walking the floor, getting your hands dirty, and using your experience to build confidence in others. When we lead by serving, we don't just solve problems—we create leaders.

Don't Take Humble and Empathetic Leadership for Granted

Empathy and humility are rare—but powerful leadership qualities. In workplaces where authority, control, and ego often take centre stage, encountering a leader who leads with compassion, kindness, and genuine understanding is a gift. And if you find yourself in such an environment—consider yourself lucky.

A humble and empathetic leader creates a space where team members feel safe to speak up, take initiative, and stretch beyond their perceived limits. In that space, innovation thrives, collaboration deepens, and people grow—not out of fear, but out of inspiration.

But let's be clear: humility is not weakness. Empathy is not a lack of strength. In fact, it takes incredible inner strength to listen deeply, stay grounded, admit mistakes, and put people before ego. These are not soft skills—they are leadership superpowers.

If you ever have the good fortune to work under such a leader, don't make the mistake of underestimating them—or worse, taking advantage of their grace. That's like playing with fire and expecting not to get burnt. Instead, leverage their presence for your own growth. Stay transparent, keep trust alive, and lean into the values they model.

Because when you align with leaders who lead from the heart, you don't just grow—you elevate.

Key Takeaways:

- Gratitude in leadership isn't just about saying "thank you"—it's about being aware of and acknowledging the quiet contributions of others.
- Servant leadership builds trust, capability, and resilience within teams.
- Leading with humility and empathy creates an environment where people feel safe to stretch and grow.
- Staying connected with your team and your purpose keeps you grounded—and effective.

Reflections:

- Who are the "Krishnas" in your leadership journey? Have you thanked them lately?
- When was the last time you descended the ladder to walk beside your team?
- How do you model gratitude, humility, and service in your daily leadership?
- Are there unrecognized contributions in your team that deserve acknowledgment?

"A leader is best when people barely know he exists. When his work is done, his aim fulfilled, they will say: we did it ourselves."

— Lao Tzu

Conclusion

Lead With Purpose, Leave a Legacy

Leadership is not a finish line—it's a lifelong journey of becoming. It's a rhythm of growth, reflection, and meaningful contribution. The 10 life philosophies described below, woven throughout this book are not abstract ideals. They are living principles—practical, powerful, and deeply personal. When practiced with intention, they shape not just the course of a leader's career, but the quality of their life. They help us become leaders who don't just manage, but inspire, elevate, and transform.

Ten Truths to Lead By:

1. **People before tasks:** Leadership begins with hearts, not checklists. The relationships we nurture give our work meaning and our mission purpose.

2. **Intent over outcome:** It's not just what you achieve, but why you act. Integrity of purpose lays the foundation for authentic impact.

3. **Excellence is non-negotiable:** Quality isn't a feature—it's a mindset. Leaders who hold the bar high invite others to rise with them.

4. **Limitations exist—possibilities abound:** Every wall has a door. Great leaders don't dwell on constraints; they explore the infinite room for innovation.

5. **Process is the path:** Obsess less about the destination and more about each step taken with care. Progress is born from the journey.

6. **Success is a rhythm, not a moment:** Celebrate milestones, yes—but never stop evolving. True success lies in sustained, purposeful movement.

7. **Be true to your calling:** Don't reflect others' expectations. Trust your voice, your vision, and the value you bring.

8. **Stay open to change:** Growth begins where comfort ends. Leaders thrive when they're humble enough to keep learning.

9. **Grow together:** Leadership isn't a solo act. Seek out the brilliance in others and let collaboration become your catalyst.

10. **Lead with gratitude:** A grateful heart grounds a soaring mind. Pause. Appreciate. What you have today was once something you hoped for.

By living these principles, we lead not from authority, but from authenticity. Leadership isn't about position—it's about presence. It's about how we show up, how we listen, how we leave people better than we found them. When we lead with humility, curiosity, and compassion, we create space for others to grow—and in doing so, we grow ourselves.

As we close this chapter, let nature remind us: everything that thrives adapts. Just as the seasons shift and rivers find new paths, we too must evolve. Leadership is not static; it's a living expression of who we are becoming. Let each day be a step toward the best version of yourself.

Remember: life isn't about perfection—it's about meaningful progress. When we strive to simplify, to improve, to uplift—we don't just succeed, we inspire.

So go forth:

- Lead with love.
- Stand in integrity.
- Move with gratitude.
- Let your presence inspire, and your absence be felt.

That is the legacy worth leaving.

> *"Leadership is not about titles or power; it is about the quiet strength to inspire, the humility to serve, and the courage to grow—each day, with purpose, integrity, and a heart full of gratitude."*
>
> *– From the author*
> *– Dr. Subhashis Chakraborty*

Letter to Future Leaders

Dear Future Leader,

If you're reading this, it means you've chosen a path that's not always easy—but always meaningful. Leadership, as you've seen through these pages, is not about control, prestige, or being the loudest in the room. It's about showing up—authentically, intentionally, and courageously—for yourself and for others.

There will be days when doubt whispers louder than confidence. Moments when you're expected to have answers but carry only questions. Times when your principles are tested in silence, not spectacle. In those moments, remember this: leadership is not a destination; it is a daily decision.

Choose to lead with empathy, even when it feels inconvenient. Choose to listen more deeply when the noise is high. Choose to create leaders around you, not followers behind you. Your actions will inspire far more than your instructions ever will.

Let your leadership be grounded in gratitude, fuelled by purpose, and shaped by service. Stay curious. Stay human. Stay committed to touching the core—your own and that of those you serve.

Because the world doesn't just need more leaders. It needs more true ones!

With respect and belief in you,

– Dr. Subhashis Chakraborty